Speak Up!
& Succeed

SECOND EDITION

Pegasus Media World
Los Angeles, California orders@pegasusmediaworld.com PegasusMediaWorld.com

Speak Up! & Succeed: How to Get Everything You Want in Meetings, Presentations and Conversations
© 2007, 2019. Nance Rosen. All Rights Reserved.

Cover design, book interior design and prepress production by Tethos Creative, tethos.com

ISBN, print ed. 978-0-9786078-6-9
ISBN, ebook ed. 978-0-9786078-7-6
ISBN, audio ed. 978-0-9786078-8-3

First Printing 2007
Revised Edition First Printing 2019

Unattributed quotations are by Nance Rosen. Anecdotes and profiles of well-known individuals cited are true to the best knowledge of the author at this time. In keeping with the HBR case approach, examples contained within the writing reflect actual and common communication and managerial challenges and offer direct expressions of effective solutions, while the names of the speakers and companies along with certain details have been fictionalized where necessary to protect their identities.

Library of Congress Cataloging-in-Publication Data
Rosen, Nance.
Speak Up! And Succeed: How To Get Everything You Want In Meetings, Presentations And Conversations / Nance Rosen. – 2nd ed.
p. cm.
Includes index.
LCCN 2007932543
ISBN-13: 978-0-9786078-6-9 (print ed.)
1. Success in business. I. Title.
2. Business communication.
3. Oral communication.
4. Interpersonal communication.
R674 2007
650.1'3
QBI07-600197

Nance Speaks!

Speak Up!
& Succeed

SECOND EDITION

NANCE ROSEN

For my daughter

Molly Jo,

to whom I owe everything

NANCE ROSEN

Why Read This Book?

IT'S BEEN SAID THAT SOME OF THE GREATEST MUSICIANS IN THE WORLD have never played a note—because they never knew they had the talent. Someone could have perfect pitch their entire lives, and never take advantage of it.

Similarly, you could have the greatest ideas in the world. But if you can't put them into words—if you can't get them out on the table—if you aren't able to be heard and understood by the people who make the decisions—those great ideas will die inside of you, without ever having the chance to rise up and shine.

I know something about this. My name is Peter Shankman, and I've given over 2,500 keynotes to corporations all around the world, on six continents. I've spoken to heads of state, I've spoken to Fortune 10 CEOs. I've started and sold three companies, the most recent one being a company that fundamentally changed how journalists and sources interacted.

Yet, none of that would have been even remotely possible, if I hadn't learned to voice my ideas, if I hadn't learned to speak up, and if I hadn't known how to put my thoughts into actionable verse when it came down to my moment to shine. Without knowing that, I wouldn't be even remotely as successful as I am.

That's why *Speak Up and Succeed*, is so important. In today's social and technological age, where the average attention span is 2.7 seconds, you've got one shot—roughly 160 characters, to get your words out, powerfully, and accurately, to the people who matter. Until you can do that, nothing else matters.

Read this book. Nance Rosen has put together the ultimate primer for those who want to succeed. Whether you get tongue-tied on a daily basis or speak to the world multiple times a week, there is gold in these pages.

It's time to take what you say to the next level—and beyond.

PETER SHANKMAN
shankman.com
New York, NY

Table of Contents

    i Why Read This Book?

  vii Foreword

    x Acknowledgments

    1 Introduction

7 Section One

The Key Concepts Behind the Speak Up System

11 Chapter 1: Success and Failure

17 Chapter 2: The Power of an Outcome Mind

23 Chapter 3: Communication Leadership

29 Chapter 4: Misery Triggers

35 Chapter 5: Trigger Talk

41 Section Two

The Speak Up System Overview

45 The Speak Up System Cheat Sheet

49 Chapter 6: Overview of The Speak Up System

57 Section Three

The Speak Up System in Action

61 Chapter 7: Persuasive Presentation

69 Chapter 8: Training Presentation

75 Chapter 9: Team Presentation

81 Chapter 10: Briefing Presentation

The Speak Up System

89 Section Four

Act 1, Segment 1 (Introduce Yourself)

93 Chapter 11: Heroic Achievement

97 Chapter 12: Startling Statistics

103 Chapter 13: Dramatic Quotation

107 Section Five

Act 1, Segment 2 (Introduce Your Topic)

111 Chapter 14: Crime Story

115 Chapter 15: Epidemic Statistic

119 Chapter 16: Nugget

123 Chapter 17: Example or Analogy

127 Chapter 18: Success Story

133 Section Six

Act 1, Segment 3 (Make Promises)

137 Chapter 19: Promises

149 Section Seven

Act 2, Segment 1 (Foster Understanding)

153 Chapter 20: Logic, Demos, Insights

159 Section Eight

Act 2, Segment 2 (Create Belief)

163 Chapter 21: Comparisons, Downsides, Credibility, Inspiration

171 Section Nine
Act 2, Segment 3 (Ignite Urgency)
175 Chapter 22: Interactivity, Tips, Accountability

183 Section Ten
Act 3, Segment 1 (Recall Promises Kept)
187 Chapter 23: Recall Promises Kept

191 Section Eleven
Act 2, Segment 3 (Add Unexpected Value)
195 Chapter 24: Tangible Gifts
201 Chapter 25: Intangible Gifts

207 Section Twelve
Act 3, Segment 3 (Give Instructions)
211 Chapter 26: Action & Commitments

221 Appendix
Helpful Resources
223 Library of Success
229 The Four Dimensions of Decision-Making
235 More Assets
237 Index

241 About Nance Rosen

Foreword

SOMEONE ONCE TOLD ME THAT THE ONLY PEOPLE WHO ACTUALLY READ the foreword of a book are flipping pages *before* buying it. I hope that's true, and that you haven't yet bought this book, but are considering doing so. In just a second, I am going to ask you to stop reading and perform a short exercise. Based on the outcome of that exercise, I am going to suggest that you take one of two actions: either a) put this book back where you found it; or b) move immediately to the checkout aisle (or checkout button, if you're scanning the first few pages of this book online) so you can make an essential investment in your future.

Ready? Here's the exercise.

Go to the Table of Contents and read the title and key points of each chapter. As you read the words, ask yourself a simple question: "Could I learn anything important or useful from this chapter?" If you come up with even one "no" answer, then you shouldn't buy this book.

Instead, you should put it back on the shelf (whether that shelf is virtual or three-dimensional) . . . because you are, alas, a victim of pre-judgment—the mental and spiritual epidemic of our day, and the cause of innumerable business-shattering, relationship-shattering and self-esteem-shattering pieces of "received wisdom," usually about what *can't* be done.

Each and every chapter in this book has the ability to change the way you think—*if you let it*. Changing thoughts changes outcomes. But in order to benefit from Nance Rosen's magnificent, career-altering, life-changing ideas, which abound in the pages that follow, you'll need to believe you have success coming to you. In other words, you'll need to empty your mind's painful memories of failure and rejection into your trash bin. That means getting rid of each and every thought that vaguely resembles any of the following formulations:

"I've already tried something like *that*."

"*That* will never work in our marketplace."

"My manager will never allow *that* to happen."

"We can't do *that* because _____."

That's the sound of prejudgment. That's the sound of self-sabotage disguised as wisdom. Unless you can get past those thoughts, you won't benefit from what follows in this extraordinary book.

If you want the right to buy this book, you must buy into it and replace any and all of these prejudging responses with the belief that you have a right to get beyond whatever is keeping you down.

That's right: get over yourself. Clear your mind entirely of negativity.

While you're at it, obliterate every single thought that has anything close to a "can't" theme. Drop the apostrophe "t"! You can do this!

On the fence? If you still don't know whether you've got the right to buy this book, take a moment right now to compose a single simple sentence in your mind, about your world, using this precious moment of yours, which is your most valuable resource: a chunk of time you will never get back. Let's use it now!

Make sure this one brand-new sentence you are composing right now accurately describes, in a positive way, the goal or outcome that you want to create in your business, career or personal life as a direct result of reading this book. Again: make it a positive statement!

If you're tempted to make your sentence sound like this:

"I must stop wasting my time trying to sell to people who can't buy."

Revise it in your mind so that it sounds like this:

"I'm ready for the right method to get me what I want from everyone who can buy, approve, take instructions or otherwise do exactly what I desire."

On your mark, get set—go! Got it? Excellent.

Now, SAY YOUR SENTENCE OUT LOUD, with only positive energy and a firm belief that you've earned the right to succeed. If people stare at you there in the aisle of the bookstore, so much the better: Now you have evidence that you've got a fresh start and a powerful outcome in mind, and hence the right to buy this book.

Seriously. Did you compose the sentence and say it out loud? If so, head quickly for the checkout lane (or push the "checkout now" button).

Did you compose the sentence in your head and wish you had the courage to say it out loud? OK, you pass. You're on the right track, and Nance will make sure you arrive at your destination.

Did you think, "What a stupid idea—stating your goal in positive terms. I'm not going to bother with this?"

Put this book down immediately! It's not for you.

One last thought. If you've made the cut and received my permission, I want you to make a commitment to attack this book physically.

You read right. I want you to highlight, underscore, dog-ear, page-mark, footnote and otherwise call attention to each and every idea in this book that directly supports the goal that you just came up with. Before you've finished this book, you will be able to turn all of Nance's golden concepts into a personal action plan . . . and have the skills to work that plan until you overachieve the goal you just came up with!

Welcome to a world of endless possibilities!

ANTHONY PARINELLO
Author of *Selling to VITO*
and *Think and Sell Like a CEO*

Acknowledgments

MY MOTHER, BLOSSOM ROSEN, WAS THE FIRST STAR I SAW UP CLOSE AND personal. After raising our family on $400 a month and a lot of ingenuity, she entered business when I entered college. She became the highest-paid sales representative in the apparel industry and then a business owner with no equal when it comes to integrity and ethics.

My daughter, Molly Jo Rosen, remains my greatest inspiration. She is the most courageous person I have ever known. She has overcome obstacles to create a life that is filled with setting and getting goals, plus she is crazy beautiful.

Numerous individuals have given me insight, direction, opportunity, and support. At this writing, I want to express my appreciation to Jon Torerk CSCS, Julie Lippincott Bodine, Van Anderson, Ryan Rusnak, Michael Ross, Heidi Cunningham, Wes Lambert, Robert Bargamin, Lauraine Gustafson, Helen Kim, Rebecca Fabbri, David Tseng, Andra Vaccaro, John Bwarie, Robert Eddy, Bobby Borg, Claire Belzidsky, Leticia Ng, UCLA and UCLA Extension.

This book and my career as a keynote speaker and trainer in business communication and marketing are a direct result of the amazing opportunities I experience as an educator in several academic institutions, especially at the UCLAx business and management continuing executive education program. At these academic institutions and by invitation to speak at companies, trade associations, and business summits around the world, I have trained tens of thousands of individuals who are actively using the strategies you are about to master. My students are found at the senior level of Global 2000 companies, small entrepreneurial firms, consulting and professional firms, and philanthropic and cause-based organizations. They are also at the entry-level and mid-level, and in a full range of jobs and departments. It is the feedback from these achievers, especially their reports from the field and questions about specific challenges they face, that has deeply informed my thinking and the evolution of my approach to communication, marketing, and outcome planning.

Of course, I stand on the shoulders of giants, including Anthony Parinello, Emanuel Schegloff, Martin Kaufman, Allan Jacobs, Bob Polik, Peter Shankman, Jim Collins, Michael Ray, and Laurel Mellin.

A great well of gratitude goes to my career coaching clients and the client companies I train at NanceSpeaks.com. Thank you to CNBC, who named me "America's Top Job Coach" and the 420 media outlets that have featured my work on career transitions, job hunting, success, communication, personal branding, business development, and marketing.

Lastly, I want to express my appreciation to all the broadcasters, talk show hosts, news anchors, and reporters who deliver information in a way that holds our attention and gets us to take action. Thank you for being my constant companions as I prepared this book, promoted it, and continue to improve my own communication.

Introduction

I WANT YOU TO GET EXACTLY WHAT YOU WANT: WHAT YOU REALLY, REALLY want.

WHAT ARE YOU WAITING FOR?

Whatever you want is out there, waiting for you to come and get it.

To speed you along your path to success, I've created, tested, and perfected the SPEAK UP SYSTEM.

This book is all about your getting exactly what you want, what you really, really want—as rapidly as humanly possible. I stress the human part because success is a two-part equation.

SMART ACTIONS + QUALITY INTERACTIONS = SUCCESS

Part one of the success equation is about you and you alone. You must do your best as you produce the stuff of work: reports, research, bids, spreadsheets, designs, programs, and the like.

Part two of the success equation is all about how you deal with other people. How good are you at getting other people to do what you want?

Do you fully understand the role these other people play in your life? They can say "yes," produce what you need, agree to the schedule you want, write the check, and go above and beyond their job descriptions for you. In a thousand different ways, they can accelerate your progress and speed up your journey to success. You cannot succeed without them, and you will not get to enjoy the wildly happy and satisfied life you deserve unless they feel driven to help you along your path. Communicating and collaborating with other people is what this book is about.

I wrote this book because, after years in business with some of the world's largest companies, including The Coca-Cola Company and other Global 2000 organizations, entrepreneurial environments, and associations including The Medical Marketing Association, I had to leave business. To most people, it seemed I left for great opportunities in media and academia, but I really felt an urgency to leave for one reason. I had to get a grip on why everyone was so miserable at work. Almost everyone I spoke with—people at industry gatherings, strangers on airplanes, friends at dinner parties—repeated the same lament. People complained about other people. It seemed almost everyone was frustrated, depressed, angry, and disturbed about the same thing: other people.

The stories varied, but the theme was the same. It could be the jerk they worked for, the lazy co-workers they dealt with, the stalling customers who wouldn't sign orders, or the investors and bankers who wouldn't fund deals. I never heard anyone joyfully recounting a great conversation, presentation, or meeting at work.

I knew plenty of successful people, but they were suffering for that success. They were muscling their way to the top, and they were showing the signs of all that stress. I did, too. My career was like a speeding bullet. I ran a major division for one of the top two ad agencies in the US by the time I was 25. I was a director of marketing in the Fortune 500 at the age of 28. I was president of a trade association at 32. I ran my own consulting firm for 10 years, during which time we won 79% of all of the business pitches we made. I sat on the boards of several companies. I certainly enjoyed interacting with the incredibly talented, wise, and decent people I met during all those years, but after being courted and employed by the number one most recognized brand in the world, I left the business world—to everyone's surprise.

Like a professional athlete seriously injured from years in the game, I was exhausted and in pain after all my "success."

So, I took what I planned would be one year off from the fast track and got a job hosting a program called International Business on public radio. I did it for ten years, added a syndicated television program called NightCap for a couple of years and began teaching executives, entrepreneurs, engineers, and managers who were continuing their education on the campuses of UCLA and the University of California, Irvine. These business leaders and professionals then hired me to train their people on marketing, sales, negotiations, product development, leadership, and business development, and with my incredible staff, produce marketing and communications programs.

Their invitations took me around the world and brought the world to me. I now have thousands of alumni in about forty countries. I conduct summits on communications training and business development. I coach companies and individuals on strategy for growth and personal improvement.

After this decade of teaching, training, and consulting, it became apparent to me that most individuals and their organizations believe they aren't good enough at the thing they do. Is there something wrong with their marketing and sales strategy? Product development platforms or quality? Customer service? Employee retention and satisfaction programs?

Yes, sometimes there are deficiencies in products, programs, and plans. However, they are very easy to see, and the fixes are not all that hard to implement. In fact, the bigger the problem in any of these areas, the more obvious and satisfying the solution.

However, even when they make changes in systems, procedures, and products, almost every one of these individuals and companies fail to get all the success they could enjoy. Why? It is because smart action—making better products, producing better reports, understanding and targeting the market better, and managing finances—is only half of the equation for success.

The second half of the success equation is quality interaction: what people do when they are in front of their prospects, customers, superiors, subordinates, suppliers, strategic partners, investors, and other key influencers. How well they communicate—or fail to communicate—determines whether others will agree, approve, join, hire, or otherwise help them.

In most business situations, you can only succeed through speed. Your competition sees the same opportunities you do. They can copy your products and services. With a bigger marketing budget or more feet on the street or buzz online, your competition can overtake you. That is, if you only focus on your features, functions, policy, and strategy—your stuff: you will not succeed.

However, if you are better at getting people to take action, you are going to be more successful, more quickly than anyone else.

Communication leadership is the only sure way to get to the highest ground, where you can see all the choices you have. From there, you can frame the decisions other people have, giving you control. Only then, do you enjoy mastery over what you do, and how much compensation and recognition you earn.

It doesn't matter what you do for a living; success is always going to depend on your having a reliable method for getting others to do things your way, to approve the projects and plans you desire, to say "yes" when you can't afford a "no."

That's why I wrote this book. I looked at thousands of individuals and their interactions at work. I picked the ones that were most instructive, both for what they did right and what they did wrong. Then I applied the classical literature on consumer buying behavior, including my own findings in this academic and applied discipline. Finally, I developed a method that I call the Speak Up System. It's easy to use and effective, no matter what type of interaction you have. It's been tested and approved by sales representatives, engineers, managers at all levels, trainers, professionals, entrepreneurs from veterans to newbies, job hunters, and career transition seekers. After 10 years of revisions, I put all that intelligence into this book.

So, you and I are going on this journey to your success. It is my most ardent desire that you find work satisfying in all the big and small ways it has the potential to be. I want you to feel mastery, to enjoy working with people because they are enthusiastically responding to you and rapidly doing what you need them to do. I want you to migrate that mastery to others, who will see you as a role model.

If this book whets your appetite for success and you want more examples, details, expert tips and techniques, you'll find new training programs when you visit NanceSpeaks.com and MyLearningChannel.com. Plus, I hope to see you at one of my online events, speaking engagements, seminars, or workshops. I would also be delighted to participate in one of your conferences or events.

If you want expert support for your business development, public speaking, business communication, employee productivity, employee satisfaction, and human resources programs, visit NanceSpeaks.com to see how we might work together. I am always developing new training, coursework, and coaching options to help you create the strategic, tactical, and performance prowess you need to captivate your target markets, attract strategic partners, get access to investors, and create or become the motivated, satisfied, and loyal employees who carry out successful missions.

Here is what you need to know to take control of your life at work and beyond:

1. You create your future with every word you speak.
2. Every day you have the opportunity to say the one thing that will change your life.
3. The degree to which you manage yourself determines the degree you can lead others.

Master the SPEAK UP SYSTEM via the presentation strategy laid out in this book. Then, use these concepts and methods in every conversation and meeting you have, even when you are not at the front of the room as a presenter. There are no limits to success, no seat in an office, or block on an organization chart that confine your trajectory when you are empowered with the tools of communication leadership. *Speak up and succeed!*

NANCE ROSEN, MBA
Bel Air, California

Section One

The Key Concepts Behind the Speak Up System

WHAT'S IN THIS SECTION?

Chapter 1: Success and Failure

Chapter 2: Outcome Mind

Chapter 3: Communication Leadership

Chapter 4: Misery Triggers

Chapter 5: Trigger Talk

Section One
Key Concepts

In this section, you find the key concepts behind the Speak Up System. These are fundamental truths all successful communicators understand and leverage. They will help you set intentions for your career and business aspirations, no matter where you are now on the road to success.

While the Speak Up System is organized for presentations, these key concepts will also improve your performance and results in conversations and meetings. They will help you align with opportunities, overcome hurdles, and improve your reputation. You may also use these principles in crafting and responding to electronic communication, including emails, texts, posts, and every form of social media.

Section One
CHAPTER 1

Success and Failure

COMMUNICATION SKILLS ARE ESSENTIAL TO YOUR ACTUALIZATION AS a human being. You don't want to be a robot or just a "human doing." You want to build meaningful, profitable relationships that pay dividends. Plus, when you speak up effectively, your needs become part of an organization's goals. That supersizes your success quotient.

Read on to learn how to overcome bad habits that have prevented you from getting the success you deserve.

THE SUCCESS EQUATION
Smart Actions + Quality Interactions = Success

WORKING SMART IS NOT ENOUGH

Robots work smart. They are wildly productive. Endless, repetitive, specific tasks done over and over, even expertly or quickly, are not a definition of success. No one thinks of promoting a robot. No one hopes a robot will lead. No one pays a robot to think. People only pay attention to a robot when it breaks, or something goes wrong. You don't want to be a robot.

The difference between success and failure is not doing more and more work, faster and faster. When you only focus on tasks and actions you perform on-the-job, you become a human doing. You do this, and you do that. You get attention when you break down, or something goes wrong. That is not success.

The closer you get to the real you
the happier and richer you will be

YOU ARE NOT A HUMAN DOING

You want to be a fully actualized human being, recognized and rewarded by your organization, clients, and hiring managers. If you're going to grow and achieve as a human being, have more authority, visibility, and choices: you need to engage other people in meaningful conversations, presentations, and meetings.

Communication leadership is the secret to being truly successful. You cannot get ahead if you only produce a mountain of reports, spreadsheets, designs, proposals, plans, and written content.

Yes, you need to take smart actions. And, continue to build the hard skills you need on-the-job. However, only getting better at what you do, without also mastering how to communicate who you are and what you want? That will result in a loss for you and your organization.

You cannot fulfill your potential if you can only do half of what's truly required to succeed.

Communication may be the difference between success and failure to achieve your goals. Why? Because no matter what you want, you need other people to invest in your potential, follow your vision, and respond positively to your requests.

QUALITY INTERACTIONS ARE INTENTIONAL

We are going to spend some time speaking about outcomes, specifically having outcomes in mind when you engage in conversations, presentations, and meetings. The SPEAK UP SYSTEM also leverages other essential, fundamental key concepts and tactics, along with a protocol for organizing and delivering what you want to say.

Therefore, before you "meet" the SPEAK UP SYSTEM in section two of this book, you are first going to build your awareness of key concepts and tactics to help you change your attitude and behavior when it comes to communication. That will empower you to do more than mimic a successful approach to making presentations.

Learning the fundamental concepts in section one will give you the confidence to communicate in a way that encourages people to see your authentic traits and collaborate with you. So, whether you give formal presentations, or just speak up in conversations and meetings, the key concepts and tactics in section one will empower you to be clear, crisp, and compelling.

There's never going to be a time when you miss out on the opportunity to speak up, collaborate, or lead. You will always have a way to get what you want, what you really, really want.

Let's start by considering what you have been doing, that has prevented you from realizing your utmost potential and achieving your goals.

DO YOU SUFFER FROM THESE COMMON SIGNS OF FAILING TO SPEAK UP?

The following are checklists of setbacks and challenges at work, which are all the result of failing to speak up. If even one of these statements applies to you, your life will be transformed when you begin to use the SPEAK UP SYSTEM.

CEOS, OWNERS, MANAGERS, AND MARKETERS

You need the SPEAK UP SYSTEM if you:

- Revise your quarterly or annual plans because your company misses forecasts
- Avoid direct contact with customers, investors, or analysts
- Have quality problems or complaints about your products, services, or customer support
- Have distributors and retailers calling the shots on your promotion or delivery terms
- Fail to get the best price, schedule, or quality from suppliers
- Don't attract top-tier strategic partners or vendors

JOB HUNTERS AND CAREER TRANSITION SEEKERS

You need the SPEAK UP SYSTEM if you:

- Feel bored, unmotivated, stressed, or depressed
- Hate networking and meeting new people even if they could help you
- Feel confused about how to introduce yourself
- Get rejected because you are told you are not qualified
- Seem angry or irritable to co-workers, family, or friends
- Are beginning to downgrade your financial or career aspirations
- Feel you are just "hanging on"
- Don't like your job or can't get a job you would love
- Don't like or trust the people you work with
- Have personal problems interfering with your success at work

SALES REPRESENTATIVES
You need the SPEAK UP SYSTEM if you:
- Are not making your numbers (sales, commission or growth)
- Win fewer than 74% of the pitches you make
- Are competing for customers on the basis of price
- Feel disrespected by people within your company
- Can't get your team to deliver bids or technical support on time
- Can't get management's attention on a serious problem

ENGINEERS, TECHNICAL EXPERTS, STAFF, AND CONSULTANTS
You need the SPEAK UP SYSTEM if you:
- Dread speaking with customers
- Feel confused about what role you play in meetings
- Think most company meetings are a waste of time
- Feel your ideas never get the consideration they deserve
- See others get ahead while you are stuck in your job
- Miss deadlines from time to time
- Have too much work or too little work
- Have trouble working in a team
- Want to make more money by moving over to sales

TRAINERS AND EDUCATORS
You need the SPEAK UP SYSTEM if you:
- Don't know why people try to avoid your trainings or don't cooperate with you
- Know your information is crucial but lose your nerve in front of a group
- Have a tough time training veteran employees
- Don't see learners using your training or getting value from it
- Get lukewarm or negative evaluations
- Feel underappreciated or underutilized by your organization
- Have been passed over for a promotion

TEAM LEADERS AND DEPARTMENT HEADS
You need the SPEAK UP SYSTEM if you:
- Don't know how to speak with top management to get what you need
- Get commitments, but others don't follow through as promised
- Bear significant responsibility but have little authority to make decisions

- Can't motivate your team or get their cooperation
- Miss deadlines, quality, or productivity benchmarks

THESE BAD COMMUNICATION HABITS CAUSE FAILURE

If you have these bad habits, you are likely to fail. Do you:

- Like to "wing-it" and be spontaneous
- Rarely have time to prepare
- Think conversations and meetings are casual interactions
- Attend most meetings and presentations to listen and learn
- Are passive about work and career plans
- Expect people in business to take turns
- Have been trained in "active listening"
- Think speaking up is aggressive
- Believe other people know what they want without your input
- Prefer a flat organization, where consensus is valued more than leadership
- Like to get "all the facts" before you jump in with your say-so
- Like the other side to show his or her hand first in a negotiation
- Think you need a higher rank or title to speak up
- See strangers as a danger
- Like to argue

DON'T WORRY

Soon you will master the three-act SPEAK UP SYSTEM and transform your life. You will never again be trapped in a meeting, presentation, or conversation. You will not just set goals; you'll attain them by building relationships that produce the outcomes you desire.

You will be living proof that success is simple: you get it via one quality interaction after another, having taken smart actions in between.

The Power of an Outcome Mind

THE MOST ESSENTIAL PREPARATION FOR SUCCESSFUL COMMUNICATION is having an outcome in mind for your life, as well as each relationship and interaction. Outcomes focus you and speed you toward your goals.

If you have failed,
you have over-listened

THE DANGER OF AN OPEN MIND AND OVER-LISTENING

There is a dangerous myth that encourages you to have an "open mind." Despite what gurus preach, when you have an open mind, you are vulnerable to everyone else's outcome. Would you hike into a jungle with an open wound? Can you imagine what could crawl in and infect you?

An open mind puts you in danger of "over-listening." That's when other people's outcomes dominate your thoughts and actions. Then, you find yourself being inauthentic and de-motivated. You procrastinate.

When you have an outcome mind, you can enthusiastically participate in an interaction. You are ready to collaborate, which is a fundamental component of communication leadership. You take responsibility for yourself and for the role you want to play in achieving goals. Mutual gain is only possible, when you are ready to thoughtfully and authentically engage with others.

A "no" is as good as a "yes"

With an outcome mind, you see results faster, and you see when no results are possible. Your outcome serves as a truth test because you can ask simple questions. Will this interaction move me forward toward what I want? Should I revisit this opportunity when the situation is more promising?

You will be as relieved to recognize a no-win situation as you are to see a win-win situation because either allows you to take control of your time and life.

You naturally turn your attention to people who have good intentions, decision-making authority, the right-sized budgets, and unmet needs you can fulfill. That is where the real opportunity for you exists.

THE ANTIDOTE TO OVER-LISTENING IS AN OUTCOME MIND

If you do no other preparation before a conversation, presentation, or meeting, you must have an outcome in mind for that interaction. That's how to avoid over-listening and getting dragged off your path to success.

With an outcome in mind, you can focus on what matters. It's easy to decide what to say. It's easy to respond to questions, objections, or criticism. You naturally avoid unnecessary conflict and have the patience to help others get past their concerns and hesitation.

You cannot take to the open road without a destination in mind
and expect to arrive at the ideal place

You will never meet a successful person who does not know what they want. You will never be a successful person until you know what you want.

An outcome mind allows you to effectively collaborate, negotiate, and participate in helping others achieve their outcomes, without losing control of your life and time. In this chapter, you will see different types of outcomes, each having a unique role in successful communication.

IDENTIFY YOUR ULTIMATE OUTCOME

Your ultimate outcome is your highest goal, per Professor Michael Ray. It is your sweetest fruit, per author Laurel Mellin. It is what makes life meaningful for you. It is the goal that drives you to overcome resistance.

These are the big questions. What is your purpose in life? Your destination? What fulfills your destiny?

Your ultimate outcome is an authentic, highly personal goal
It's how you want to feel about yourself

THE POWER OF YOUR ULTIMATE OUTCOME

To learn a new way of speaking and behaving when you are with other people, you need the inner strength of personal motivation. Your ultimate outcome and its allure are what will drive you to learn this new system of communication and use it when it feels strange.

How you feel about yourself is like a cold: it's contagious

WHAT VALUES DEFINE THE AUTHENTIC YOU?

When you accept and respect yourself, others do as well. You get their attention. You engage in meaningful interactions. You are goal-oriented. You are confident, consistent, clear, and compelling. That makes you irresistible.

You become a communication leader because you are speaking and listening from an immutable, powerful, and positive sense of self. You are not pushy, nagging, bragging, or annoying. You are resilient, collaborative, joyful, and attractive.

When you speak from your authentic values, nothing stops you from moving toward the destination you desire. You find a way to collaborate, accommodate, and participate with others appropriately.

YOUR PERSONAL BRAND TRIAD

My research shows your awareness of three personal dimensions creates a foundation of success in business and communication. I have an extensive assessment for identifying your personal brand triad, along with how to enhance your reputation using it, but here are the basic questions.

1. **Your Forever Dimension:** What quality has always described your true nature and always will?
2. **Your Driver Dimension:** What quality describes how you solve problems and get results?
3. **Your Helper Dimension:** What quality describes why other people want to have you around?

VALUES AND QUALITIES

Take a look at the list below, drawn from 75 years of psychological studies. What values or qualities define the authentic you and form your personal brand triad? That's what you want other people to see and feel every time you communicate.

LIST OF PERSONAL BRAND VALUES

- Wise
- Intelligent
- Philosophical
- Logical
- Objective
- Systematic
- Ethical
- Honest
- Principled
- Trustworthy
- Analytical
- Responsible
- Meticulous
- Efficient
- Methodical
- Calm
- Steady
- Clear-headed
- Articulate
- Sensible
- Studious
- Resourceful
- Decisive
- Skillful
- Polite
- Discreet
- Attentive
- Friendly
- Sociable
- Likable
- Pragmatic
- Persistent
- Determined

- Dependable
- Loyal
- Sympathetic
- Creative
- Artistic
- Talented
- Prepared
- Trained
- Educated
- Easy-going
- Relaxed
- Carefree
- Stylish
- Elegant
- Glamorous
- Cooperative
- Collaborative
- Deferential
- Humorous
- Interesting
- Amusing
- Curious
- Enthusiastic
- Energetic
- Versatile
- Flexible
- Dynamic
- Nice
- Good-natured
- Faithful
- Courageous
- Adventurous
- Imaginative

- Inventive
- Inquisitive
- Persuasive
- Appreciative
- Gracious
- Benevolent
- Powerful
- Strong
- Smart
- Driven
- Focused
- Ambitious
- Playful
- Entertaining
- Fun
- Passionate
- Romantic
- Idealistic
- Charming
- Charismatic
- Optimistic
- Generous
- Encouraging
- Inspiring
- Spiritual
- Compassionate
- Caring
- Daring
- Spontaneous
- Zealous
- Loving
- Kind
- Devoted

PROGRESSIVE OUTCOMES

Once you have heightened your self-knowledge and self-acceptance and crystallized your ultimate outcome, identify three progressive outcomes that lead you to achieve your goals. You might think of these three outcomes as milestones along your path to success.

- **Relationship Outcome:** the full measure of what each person or organization can help you achieve
- **Gateway Outcome:** the breakthrough in a relationship that starts the flow of money or opportunity to you
- **Proximate Outcome:** the results you want by the end of each interaction that moves you forward

Without these specific outcomes in mind, you are going to get lost. Sidetracked. You would go more slowly, have more failure, and be delayed or even denied the success you deserve. That's why you want to set up relationship maps and follow them.

CREATE RELATIONSHIP MAPS WITH LINKED INTERACTIONS

Most relationship outcomes require several planned, linked interactions to get what you ultimately desire. Each link—a conversation, meeting, or presentation—moves the relationship closer to your ideal outcome. Your links might include texts, calls, emails, and posts, too.

SAMPLE RELATIONSHIP MAP FOR BUSINESS DEVELOPMENT

The proximate outcome for each link is noted. Consider what you must plan to do, ask, or share in order to achieve the outcome in each link. THE SPEAK UP SYSTEM is organized to help you plan for success in each link.

LINK 1—CURIOSITY

Your prospect is intrigued about you, your company, or solution. They entertain the idea you might benefit them. You sense it's worth your time to continue interacting.

LINK 2—CONNECTION

You both sense you understand each other and have common ground worth further exploration.

LINK 3—INSPIRATION

You both feel energized by the possibilities of working together for mutual gain.

LINK 4—ENGAGEMENT

Your prospect feels safe to acknowledge unmet needs and discuss goals. You confirm you are speaking with the right person, one with purchasing authority and the right-sized budget.

LINK 5—COMMITMENT

Your prospect agrees to buy, approve, or take action if your solution would fulfill their needs. You set a clear goal for your collaboration or relationship. You agree on the initial steps to move toward it.

LINK 6—LEARNING AND SHARING

You support each other with valuable information. You gain and give access to resources, materials, and individuals that provide additional insights.

LINK 7—PROBLEM-SOLVING AND PLANNING

You discuss the options and alternative ways of fulfilling their needs and achieving your outcomes. You agree on the best solution, price, and implementation schedule. You reached your gateway outcome.

LINK 8—BUYING AND SELLING

Your prospect signs the agreement and generates payment. You prepare to deliver, install, or integrate your solution.

LINK 9—RECOMMENDATIONS AND REFERRALS

You keep each other informed about opportunities for upgrades and add-ons. You both actively seek to send additional business or contacts to each other. You meet to stay up-to-date. You reached your relationship outcome.

Because the SPEAK UP SYSTEM is a modular presentation format, you will see how its segments are useful in each of these links, as you learn the system. Visit NanceSpeaks.com for other helpful assets in planning your relationship maps.

CHAPTER 3

Communication Leadership

C OMMUNICATION LEADERSHIP WILL CHANGE YOUR LIFE. NO MATTER what title you have or where you sit in a room, see other people as your audience. Focus on your audience, not yourself, and you'll be on your way to becoming a communication leader.

You create your future with every word you speak

COMMUNICATION LEADERSHIP WILL CHANGE YOUR LIFE

Imagine just by using your words; you speed toward your goals. Inspire people to say yes to your requests. Follow your instructions. Cooperate. Agree with you. Follow through.

Communication leaders transparently aim for mutual gain. Their greatest strength is a collaborative, empathetic mindset that helps uncover real concerns: the pain, fears, and cravings in those around them.

Identify what really matters to your audience. Make that the basis of your delivering attractive, right-sized solutions that incorporate your goals. That's why people will say yes to you.

Communication leaders transparently balance compassion with self-interest for mutual gain

---

REAL LEADERS SOLVE REAL PROBLEMS

A sincere approach to problem identification is what's missing from most business interactions. It takes a mix of curiosity and empathy, plus calm, compassionate, confident self-control. When those qualities underlie every word you speak, you have amazingly fruitful relationships. That's how you acquire authority. Spark collaboration. Inspire.

Leadership is a mindset, not a title

For the majority of your life, you will not have a title that designates you as the actual leader. Your business card, nameplate, or email signature will not say "in-charge." Thus, you need a mindset and reliable method to influence anyone: peers, superiors, co-workers, subordinates, prospects, clients, investors, recruiters, decision-makers and others, without compromising on your goals or giving away too much in a deal.

No matter where you sit in a meeting, presentation, or conversation: confidence and curiosity elevate your status. Come prepared with two things. One: certainty about what you want, what you really, really want. Two: honest curiosity about what is hiding beneath surface problems and delay tactics like objections, demands, and requests for "just one more thing."

With this preparation, you can find many different pathways to get what you want. It's the outcome that matters, not the detours or distractions that are inevitable when you collaborate with others.

LOWER RESISTANCE, GET RESULTS

A compassionate mindset allows you to focus on others as they are, rather than in opposition to you or in some way judging you. Most people speak because they long to be "received," understood, and accepted. They want to see you demonstrate that you are tuned in. Ignore static, such as a harsh or argumentative tone. Focus on what they need.

Often when others express disagreement, objections, or even rejection, they are merely "working out loud." They are revealing their discomfort about change, which is a normal human reaction. You are likely witnessing their growth, even if their expression seems contrary.

With this growth-oriented mindset, you streamline your interactions. They involve less effort, time, conflict, stress, and arguments. It's easy to see why people would routinely prefer to hear from you, over your competition. When you are authentic, caring, and clear-spoken: you have no competition.

The degree to which you manage yourself
equals the degree you can lead others

BE AUTHENTIC, NOT VULNERABLE

Self-awareness and self-regulation are fundamental to leadership, but most people fail to leverage these essential tools of self-management. In fact, most people misuse business relationships. They mistakenly act out vulnerabilities, like the need for self-expression, admiration, and emotional support. Unfortunately, neediness overshadows positive, authentic qualities like inventiveness, bravery, and logic in business interactions.

Hobbies and side hustles should fulfill your personal passions
Work demands the motivation to satisfy the needs of others

If you have a fight, flight, or freeze reaction when you are with an audience, you simply have the wrong mindset about the purpose of interactions and work itself.

It's counter-intuitive to think about others as much as you think about yourself. Yet, it's that exact strategy that gets you exactly what you want, quickly and stress-free.

THE RULE OF RECIPROCITY
When you trust, like, and care about others,
they trust, like, and care about you

That is what the SPEAK UP SYSTEM banks on: the Rule of Reciprocity. By showing you are concerned about them, way beyond their expectations of how an ordinary human would behave, they reward you with the extraordinary benefits of being trusted, liked, and cared about. It works like magic, but it's merely human nature.

HOW TO BE CONFIDENT

Invest in yourself before you show up for others. Face the brutal truth that uncovers what you want: what you really, really want. Practice and prepare what you want to say, so when you show up, you are not improvising.

HOW TO SUCCEED

You need to establish and then build support. You need the same people to show up ready to help you, again and again. You need people to recommend you to others, so your sphere of influence and access expands. You need to build a reputation, résumé, or history that makes strangers reach out to you with lucrative, satisfying offers.

Relationships are investments that pay dividends

If you want the cascade of positive benefits that flow from relationships, you want to be a communication leader. You want to have a reliable way to locate the intersection of self-interest and compassion quickly, in every situation, at any time. You want a way to start out right with anyone, and then be able to go back, over and over, to reap more and more.

Relationships are made by making and keeping promises

A FORMULA FOR COMMUNICATION LEADERSHIP

That is what the SPEAK UP SYSTEM is. It is a way to set your intention easily, smartly plan ahead, and then confidently execute the essential elements of communication leadership, no matter what role you have now or what you aspire to do in the future. It builds secure, fruitful relationships.

The SPEAK UP SYSTEM prepares you to promise your audience they will make progress as a result of your relationship. You are ready to demonstrate compassion for their feelings. You have curiosity driving you to uncover what really matters to them. You have a set of right-sized solutions in mind. You have practiced giving instructions the audience can easily follow. Every time you meet, you demonstrate things are getting better for them.

When you prepare for any interaction using the SPEAK UP SYSTEM three-act formula, you interact with empathy and confidence. You can think less about yourself and focus more on how your audience is doing. You don't worry about improvising. You don't worry about how you might be received. You are confident and relaxed. You can be creative, humorous, intuitive, or exhibit whatever authentic qualities feel natural to you.

Most importantly, you can focus on others' needs, even while you are executing a plan to achieve your own goals and ideal outcomes.

Focus is the basis of achievement

YOU DESERVE TO STAR IN YOUR OWN LIFE

Whether you are an entrepreneur, employee, job candidate, sales representative, consultant, advocate, educator, vendor, professional, owner, coach, freelancer, intern, or volunteer: you must be the star of your own life and career.

It's not egotistical to think of yourself as a star. It's an essential element of communication leadership.

Take responsibility for your audience's experience

All stars—rock stars, celebrities, talk show hosts, and social media influencers seek to establish and deepen the connection audiences feel for them. They take responsibility for the relationship because they know they need audiences to support them, follow them, repeatedly tune-in, and purchase from them, plus evangelize to others.

Stars understand audiences have a lot of distractions and choices about how to spend their time and money. So, stars leverage their authentic talent to present maximally attractive and authentically engaging experiences for their audiences.

By the time stars perform, they are not worried about themselves. They focus entirely on delivering the ideal audience experience.

TAKE CARE OF YOUR AUDIENCE

You must see yourself as a star and the people around you as your audience. That will remind you to take responsibility for the relationships you have or want to initiate. That will remind you to focus on the audience, while you confidently leverage your authentic nature and talents.

All speaking is public speaking
There is no casual conversation

Whether you are speaking to one person in a conversation, a dozen in a meeting, thousands in a presentation, or millions on a broadcast: treat other people as your audience. Do not expect them to imagine what would be good for you, what you could do for them, or how you can work together successfully.

Prepare to get results with your audience

THIS IS BUSINESS, NOT SHOW BUSINESS

All communication in the workplace is a public engagement, but it is not naked self-expression of your unique talent. Prepare to be a safe, nourishing presence for your audience, even while you are an advocate of your own goals, solutions, and point of view.

Collaboration is the intersection of mutual gain

Your clarity, curiosity, compassion, and confidence are what lead to a meaningful and often joyful collaboration that serves you and your audience. It is the only ethical, legitimate use of time in business. It gets decisions that stick.

You will never again have the misimpression that "they said yes" or "they seemed interested," only to find they don't call you back, won't take your calls or don't do what they promised they would.

WHY THE SPEAK UP SYSTEM WORKS

In the simplest terms, the bulk of the SPEAK UP SYSTEM is gaining an audience's "know-like-ignite" response to you and your products or services.

When you facilitate an audience to reveal their real needs, patiently frame a solution set, and guide them to select the right-sized one: you have demonstrated communication leadership.

CHAPTER 4

Misery Triggers

A N AUDIENCE RARELY TELLS YOU THE TRUTH AND YOU CAN ASSUME YOU will find deeper problems that need mining once you establish trust. You'll need to arm yourself with misery triggers: what causes real pain, fear, and craving in your audience to help them identify the root cause of their dissatisfaction.

For every complex problem
there are many superficial distractions

ANTICIPATE A DEPTH DEFICIT

Very few people tell the truth. Expect them to be evasive and non-committal, until they feel confident they can trust you. They might share surface complaints. They may indicate everything's fine. They might even boast things could not be better.

Expect a lot of false assertions. Many will be distractions, unrelated to real problems that need solving.

Don't run out the clock by over-listening or over-sharing during small talk. If you take too much time with superficial chatter, your relationship may remain superficial. You want to use your time and life effectively.

The basis of a real business relationship involves mining your audience for misery: their genuine pain, fear, and craving. Until you uncover the source of their suffering, you cannot collaborate on the right-sized solution.

THE DISSATISFACTION GAP
The distance between real life and the ideal life

LOOK FOR THE GAP

Everyone has a gap between their real life and their ideal life. Every organization has problems they yearn to overcome. Your audience needs to bridge the distance between how things are now and how they would like them to be. You want to be the bridge or at least help build it.

Listen for symptoms of their misery. With empathy and honest curiosity, ask what they think is causing it. That is a safe place to start mining for facts that reveal the real, often complex problems they face.

SYMPTOMS OF MISERY

- Worry
- Irritation
- Aggravation
- Embarrassment
- Shame
- Depression
- Self-Doubt
- Anger
- Fear
- Concern
- Frustration
- Disappointment
- Loathing
- Anxiety
- Nervousness
- Numbness
- Grief
- Powerlessness

WHAT IS MISERY?

Misery has three levels of decreasing urgency. Always focus on the most pressing concerns. The most urgent needs involve pain. Next, fears may present opportunities for you to offer solutions. Finally, cravings can be buying triggers. Before you can attempt to solve a problem, look for specific situations or obstacles driving an audience to feel symptoms of distress. Misery triggers come from feelings of stress about the present, distrust of the future, or discontent about staying with the status quo. Here's what you are looking for, in the order that presents the best opportunity for you.

- **Pain**—a current problem your audience finds very stressful
- **Fear**—a looming consequence your audience wishes they could avoid, delay, or disappear
- **Craving**—a yearning your audience wishes they could fulfill to enjoy more security, prestige, or happiness

Misery Trigger #1: Pain

Pain is the state of mind when a person or organization suffers a significant loss or plunges into misfortune. Pain also occurs when something previously overlooked is suddenly and urgently needed, noticeably absent, or difficult to attain.

MISERY TRIGGER #2: FEAR

Fear is the state of mind when a person or organization becomes acutely aware of a looming event likely to result in pain. Concern about potential damage in the near future causes the greatest fear, especially if the magnitude of harm is significant.

MISERY TRIGGER #3: CRAVING

Craving is the state of mind when a person or organization wants something that seems all but unattainable. Longing or yearning is amplified when fulfillment seems unlikely. Resentment and envy often accompany craving.

WHAT CAUSES MISERY?

Typical misery triggers include losing a major account (pain), facing the need for changing a system or policy (fear), or discovering a competitor reached an enviable goal (craving).

Misery triggers shine a harsh light on the gap between someone's real life and their ideal life.

TYPICAL PAIN TRIGGERS

- Loss of key customers
- Loss of key personnel
- Product defects result in unexpected product returns
- Failing to meet a crucial deadline
- Out-of-control costs or expenses
- Cutbacks in staff or resources
- Failing to reach a forecast
- Loss of income
- Losing an important channel of distribution
- Equipment breakdown or plant shutdown
- Failure in systems, infrastructure, or processes
- Disagreements or agreements falling through
- Product, prototype, clinical trial, or pilot program failure
- Closure ordered by regulators or authorities
- Penalties or fines levied

TYPICAL FEAR TRIGGERS

- Competitors release new, more desirable products or services
- Competitors recruit a key customer or key individual
- Suppliers raise prices or create supply problems
- A deadline looms and is nearly impossible to meet
- Regulators deliver a warning or impose a probationary status
- Product defects suddenly rise
- Aging information systems begin to overload and slow
- Unexpected costs or expenses crop up
- Customer complaints rise
- A forecast is about to be missed
- Market share or visibility shrinks
- Negative publicity or rumors arise
- Loss of an exclusive or valuable relationship with a channel or outlet
- Experiencing an unexpected downgrade in status or access
- Poor results from prototypes or initial stages of pilot programs
- An audit notice or inquiries from regulators or authorities
- Threats of penalties or fines for being out of compliance

TYPICAL CRAVING TRIGGERS

- Others receive rewards for accomplishment
- Peers excel and enjoy status symbols or publicity
- Competition arises for recognition or reward
- Competitors make an unexpected gain
- Competitors prevail, and the loss hurts
- Loss of recognition, compensation, or authority
- Being forced to cope with a lack of variety or constant routine
- Personnel outgrows the circumstances or position
- A crushing workload or excessive responsibility without authority
- Working with poorly functioning systems, equipment, or tools
- An ongoing shortage of resources or help
- Being denied or rejected after making a request
- Experiencing a little bit of success or status without a roadmap for more
- Sudden loss of status, prestige, or recognition
- Others receive upgrades or additional resources
- Popular culture or business mores signal new norms
- Making a bid or submitting a quote for something highly desirable

MISERY JUMPSTARTS ENGAGEMENT

Sensitively focus your audience on their misery. You may need to gently amplify it, to focus them on why it needs to be resolved, and ignite their desire to collaborate with you.

Discuss the potential implications of not taking action. Investigate the root causes or hidden factors that lurk behind the problems they see.

This is not a call for you to prod them much beyond their comfort zone. No one likes to be forced into confronting the brutal truth. Be sensitive to their capacity for change. Assess whether they have the required motivation, commitment, and resources. SPEAK UP SYSTEM presentations are organized that way.

ASK EMPATHETIC QUESTIONS

With honest curiosity, you can enlarge their dissatisfaction gap and come to an accurate assessment of the problem. You might ask:

1. How did this happen?
2. What will happen if the problem goes unresolved?
3. How many more incidents will likely crop up?
4. Who else will be affected?

You cannot make money before you make meaning

The problem identification stage is an opportunity for you to showcase the value you bring to the collaboration. Provide a success story or example that expands their aspirations. Share trends or forecasts to show looming consequences for those clinging to the status quo.

You have a lot of competition if you are just taking orders. However, you create a unique position in the mind of your audience when you respectfully demonstrate your expertise or provide insights that go beyond surface issues or requirements. That's how you eradicate your competition.

SCOPE OUT THE RIGHT-SIZED SOLUTION

Once you have collaborated to identify the real problem and its consequences, you can move toward your outcome. The ideal way to present your solution is by creating a set of three alternatives, what we call a "3-set."

THE GOLDILOCKS PRINCIPLE
too big, too small, just right

Without showing scorn for your competition or disdain for alternative solutions, you can address competing approaches as being perfect for other situations—just not the one your audience is facing right now. Alternatively, if you have a portfolio of solutions that you provide, you can present them as being good, better and best. Lastly, you might show a solution set with 1) an easy, low-risk trial, 2) the most popular option, and 3) a premium version with the most features or support.

This 3-set approach engages your audience in making a choice within your solution set rather than feeling forced into agreeing or disagreeing with you. It helps to have examples that reflect why others made each choice, so your audience can identify what factors led to their decisions. That allows you to lead the communication and continue collaborating, rather than delivering a hard sell.

Trigger Talk

T HE MORE PREPARED YOU ARE, THE MORE SUCCESSFUL YOU WILL BE. You can listen empathetically, speak up strategically, and most importantly, you can say what you mean in a crisp, clear, and compelling way. Trigger talk is being prepared to deliver your stories, examples, and content effortlessly. It is essential to communication leadership.

Improvisation is the fastest way to fail

SAVE YOUR ENERGY

When you respect your audience and your outcomes, you do not freestyle. Improvising takes you inward, searching your brain, forming thoughts, and feeling your emotions. That clouds your ability to engage in collaboration and lead the communication.

Even the best-trained actors and speakers cannot face an audience without the right words on trigger, ready to deliver in the appropriate tone and pace. When you take responsibility for your audience's experience, you prepare in every way possible. The lowest threshold of readiness is equipping yourself with relevant stories, examples, and content.

Trigger talk is when you have content ready to deliver. It is an essential element of self-control. Remember, the degree to which you manage yourself determines the degree you can lead others.

WHAT YOU NEED ON TRIGGER

If you are giving a TED Talk, you need fourteen minutes of presentation memorized. Your prepared text must be so ingrained in your brain you can do other tasks while you are giving your speech. For example, you could wash dishes while watching television as the words just fall out of your mouth.

Moreover, you can do it using the pitch, pace, and volume you intend to use in front of your audience.

That extreme level of preparation and rehearsal is not likely to be what you need when you speak up in business. Often you will be listening and engaging your audience, rather than standing and delivering. So, having one long monologue memorized will not always serve you.

CHUNK IT UP

What you need on trigger are chunks of content and key phrases. For example, you want to memorize the two or three sentences you are going to use to introduce yourself. Get your examples and stories on trigger. Craft and memorize your answers to frequently asked questions.

Communicate authentically, not emotionally

The more you have on trigger, the less you have to use your brain to make sure you are making sense when you are with your audience. Trigger talk reduces your reactivity, ensuring that unwanted emotions like anxiety and irritation are not leaking out.

When you take time in advance to craft and practice, your content will not just be factually correct. It should reflect your authentic qualities. For example, if your personal brand triad is smart, inventive, and encouraging: your content will reflect those qualities along with the information you are purveying. You will confidently represent yourself.

BE READY TO SUCCEED

Write down a first draft. Add in the right adjectives, details, and emphasis. Say it out loud. Polish it. Practice it.

Look at the Library of Success for a list of content components you might craft to use in any conversation, presentation, or meeting. The Speak Up System has nine segments with formulas you can use to organize content most effectively to articulate your key points during a presentation.

Plus, look at this list of what successful people often have on trigger, depending on their situation. For example, anticipate questions from people you encounter at networking events. Consider crafting responses and getting them on trigger.

- What do you do?
- What is your background?
- Where are you from?
- What is your greatest success?
- When have you failed and what did you learn from it?
- What do you do for fun?

GET READY WITH GHOST CONVERSATIONS

During your preparation to deliver content, speak out loud as if you were in front of your audience. Otherwise, you will be shocked by the sound of your voice. Have "ghost conversations," where you envision and "hear" your interaction.

It may be ideal to practice this give and take while you are otherwise engaged. You might have a ghost conversation while you are driving or exercising to normalize interactions. Anchor them to the times in your life when you are in control because that's how you want to feel with an audience.

RESISTANCE IS COLLABORATION

Objections are a part of a collaboration. When you are calm and confident about speaking, you can feel equally relaxed and self-assured about receiving your audience's input. You merely listen empathetically, assist in identifying problems, amplify gaps you can fill, help determine a set of right-sized solutions, and generally respond compassionately rather than react emotionally.

Communication leaders understand most objections are a sign of trust. Your audience is "working out loud," so you can help them figure out how to do what you recommend. When you embrace this type of resistance as collaboration, you minimize conflict.

Objections are Collaboration
"I'm not ready."
"This is wrong."
"It's too much money."

FEEDBACK IS REALLY FEED-IN

As a communication leader facilitating a collaboration, you see all feedback as valuable. Consider what your audience says—endorsing or objecting—as merely "feed-in." They are not reacting to you. They are adding to the collaboration with their thoughts and feelings. You have done something right if your audience shares their objections, rather than just shutting down the interaction.

> *"The true character and intellectual strength of a real leader is displayed when they communicate with others, especially those with whom they disagree."* —Mark Hertling

---

Feed-in is a gift
Receive it with appreciation

PAW THEM

By responding to any feed-in with a positive acknowledgment word (PAW), you give yourself time to process the meaning and importance of their response. Put your PAW "on trigger," ready to say without thinking.

Choose your PAW and practice it. Ideally, you will have three PAWs on trigger since your audience will often repeat themselves in an effort to be received. Each time you hear the feed-in, your first response should be a PAW.

PAWs increase your status as a communication leader. The person who gives positive regard is in charge.

Sample PAWs

Great   Thank you
Super   Got it
Awesome   Brilliant

TAKE TIME BEFORE RESPONDING

The most respectful, collaborative response will show you have received your audience. Plus, you may want to slow down the velocity of emotional reactions or reflexive negativity. Put some air between receiving and responding.

When you need some time to consider your audience's feed-in, you should have three magic words on trigger.

Tell me more

LISTEN STRATEGICALLY

Consider what the objection means, beyond its literal terms. Is your audience expressing fear? Are they telling you they are not the decision-maker? Are they indicating there is more background information they need to give you before you can indeed help them?

You may not need to change your "ask" because you face resistance. You may just need to reflect you received it, using a PAW. Then, consider if it's an ideal time to continue engaging.

It might be the right moment to collaborate on what you will do in the next link and what you both need to do as actions in between now and then. If so, close this interaction by making a commitment about how you will use your next time together.

Section Two

The Speak Up System Overview

WHAT'S IN THIS SECTION?

Speak Up System Cheat Sheet

Chapter 6: Speak Up System Overview

Section Two
Key Concepts

YOU ARE ABOUT TO PUT THE KEY CONCEPTS YOU JUST LEARNED INTO ACTION! In this section, you see a remarkable, proven method for delivering powerful, transformative, and engaging presentations. Use this system to persuade, train, inspire teamwork, or provide a briefing to any audience. In essence, whenever you need to succeed, use the SPEAK UP SYSTEM presentation format.

This section starts with a "cheat sheet" outlining the three acts and nine segments that comprise the SPEAK UP SYSTEM. The cheat sheet helps you quickly structure a presentation. You see the ideal outcome plus the response your content needs to elicit from your audience in each segment. After the cheat sheet, you'll find a more descriptive overview of the system so you'll understand the function of each act and segment.

When you complete this section, review the annotated examples that follow. Then, review the Helpful Resources at the back of the book and visit NanceSpeaks.com to get more assets, examples, and guidance. Finally, dig into the remaining sections in this book to get precise instructions on how to build each segment of your own SPEAK UP SYSTEM presentations.

The Speak Up System Cheat Sheet

ACT ONE: YOUR GREAT OPENING

Transformation: Get Attention

S<small>EGMENT</small> O<small>NE</small>: I<small>NTRODUCE</small> Y<small>OURSELF</small>
Outcome: Inspire confidence
Response: *"Wow! I feel lucky to listen to you!"*

S<small>EGMENT</small> T<small>WO</small>: I<small>NTRODUCE</small> Y<small>OUR</small> T<small>OPIC</small>
Outcome: Connect with misery triggers
Response: *"Wow! I need to hear more!"*

S<small>EGMENT</small> T<small>HREE</small>: M<small>AKE</small> P<small>ROMISES</small>
Outcome: Establish your relationship
Response: *"Wow! This will empower me!"*

ACT TWO: YOUR STREAMLINED CONTENT
Transformation: Incite "Know-Like-Ignite"

SEGMENT ONE: FOSTER UNDERSTANDING
Outcome: Objectively inform or update
Response: *"Wow! Now I fully understand!"*

SEGMENT TWO: CREATE BELIEF
Outcome: Show your solution is ideal
Response: *"Wow! I like your solution the best!"*

SEGMENT THREE: IGNITE URGENCY
Outcome: Present an incentive to take action
Response: *"Wow! I don't want to miss out!"*

ACT THREE: YOUR GREAT CLOSING
Transformation: Get Action and Commitments

SEGMENT ONE: RECALL PROMISES KEPT
Outcome: Deepen your relationship
Response: *"Wow! You did exactly as promised!"*

SEGMENT TWO: OFFER UNEXPECTED VALUE
Outcome: Trigger the Rule of Reciprocity
Response: *"Wow! I feel indebted to you!"*

SEGMENT THREE: GIVE INSTRUCTIONS AND GET ACTION
Outcome: Get results and future commitments
Response: *"Wow! I am meeting my goals!"*

CHAPTER 6

Overview of
The Speak Up System

THE SPEAK UP SYSTEM USES THREE ACTS TO HELP YOU EASILY BUILD powerful presentations. Use it to transform audiences with resistant mindsets into engaged collaborators seeking mutual gain.

The Speak Up System is your "backbone of success"

THE SYSTEM FRAMEWORK

The SPEAK UP SYSTEM uses three acts in a precise order to build presentations. Act One is your Great Opening. Act Two is your Streamlined Content. Act Three is your Great Closing.

Each act includes three segments. Each segment has a specific "job" in the presentation. They work best in the order you find them. There are alternative ways to construct each segment, so you always have fresh and effective ways to use your time with an audience. The book provides detailed information about the segments along with their formulas.

SPEAK UP SYSTEM presentations are built in a modular fashion, so you can re-use segments you build. You can easily construct new segments using the formulas. Once you learn how to use the system for presentations, you can select individual acts or segments as the basis for productive conversations and meetings, as well as social media. Thus, you can successfully deploy the system in total or in part for every link along a relationship map.

Most importantly, rely on the system's ability to transform any audience from a resistant, indifferent, or oppositional mindset to one that is eager to follow your lead and take action as you desire. You'll have the power to address any issue, situation or audience. Hence, like a good backbone: the SPEAK UP SYSTEM is a sturdy skeleton that allows for fluid, forward motion.

THE TRANSFORMATION CHANNEL

The SPEAK UP SYSTEM mirrors the method marketers use to transform indifferent or resistant viewers into enthusiastic, loyal buyers. Marketing messages take an audience through specific stages of transformation, which we harness into the three acts of a presentation. You quickly gain attention. Then, you incite understanding, belief, and urgency. Lastly, you get the audience to take action and make future commitments.

SPEAK UP SYSTEM	TRANSFORMATIONAL CHANNEL
Act One: Your Great Opening ➡	Attention
Act Two: Streamlined Content ("Know-Like-Ignite") ➡	Foster Understanding, Create Belief, Ignite Urgency
Act Three: Your Great Closing ➡	Action

ACT ONE: YOUR GREAT OPENING

Before an audience will listen to you, you need their attention and commitment. That is the work of the first three segments of your first act. During this time, you also gain your audience's trust, as well as get them to like you and care about you. It is crucial to build this bond and rapport with your audience before you get to your content.

Act One, Segment One: Introduce Yourself

Segment One is structured to help the audience learn about your authentic qualities. You introduce yourself, whether the audience has previously met you, knows you very well, or is meeting you for the first time. You'll find formulas that guide you to speak about your values, experiences, and influences. The alternatives vary in length and directness: using a heroic achievement story, startling statistic, or dramatic quotation. So, you always take the time to appropriately give your audience some insight into your authentic qualities, background, or philosophy.

Your ideal outcome is to inspire confidence. Ideally, the refrain in your audience's brain is: "Wow! You have remarkable experience. I feel lucky to listen to you!"

Act One, Segment Two: Introduce Your Topic

Segment Two is structured to connect with your audience's misery triggers compassionately. You pinpoint why your topic is important and directly relevant to their best interests. You introduce your topic, using formulas that appropriately amplify an aspect of their pain, fear, or craving. You "tease" your upcoming content. There are formulas to help you accomplish this, using a crime story, epidemic statistic, example, analogy, nugget, or success story.

Your ideal outcome is to connect compassionately with their misery. Ideally, the refrain in your audience's brain is: "Wow! This is important! I need to hear more!"

Act One, Segment Three: Make Promises

Segment Three is structured to empower your audience. You promise an immediate, specific, short-term gain by the end of the presentation. Thus, you lock in their laser focus on the content you are about to deliver. Explicitly, you promise that by the end of your presentation they can take action to remedy the misery you introduced. It may also help them make progress in resolving their larger problems or reaching other goals.

While the promise is stated plainly in a sentence or two, it's tied to your proximate outcome (what you want from this interaction) as well as other longer-term outcomes you plan for the relationship. Hence, while this segment is simple, it requires the most planning on your part. There are three ways to state it: as a promise, guarantee, or commitment.

Your ideal outcome is to establish or deepen the relationship. Ideally, the refrain in your audience's brain is: "Wow! This will empower me to solve a significant problem in my life!"

ACT TWO: STREAMLINED CONTENT

Now that you have the audience's attention and commitment to listen to you, it's time to deliver your main points about the topic. That's the work of the next three segments. They are structured to deliver content in the order and manner that incites the "know-like-ignite" response. That is how you swiftly win hearts and minds. This structure reduces resistance and increases their compliance. You also fulfill the promise you made at the end of Act One.

ACT TWO, SEGMENT ONE: FOSTER UNDERSTANDING

Segment One is structured to help your audience gain knowledge relevant to your topic. You are establishing yourself as a trustworthy advisor here, so no selling. Use reliable, new, well-sourced information. The goal is to lay the groundwork for what they need to know, to develop a preference for your solution, and take the action you plan for the end of your presentation.

In the Library of Success, you may find particularly useful content components in these sections: Logic, Demonstrations, and Insights.

Your ideal outcome is to inform or update them objectively. The ideal refrain in your audience's brain is: "Wow! Now I fully understand the situation!"

ACT TWO, SEGMENT TWO: CREATE BELIEF

Segment Two is structured to instill the belief your solution or approach is best. Again, this is not a hard sell. You guide the audience through inspiring stories or different choices, options, and alternatives, leveraging their new or updated understanding of their situation. You may even explore downsides or risks inherent in these alternatives. Characterize your solution, so it is the most ideal for this audience, without denigrating competing choices. The most powerful way to create belief in your solution is to show how competing options are better for other people, who face different challenges or conditions than your audience does.

In the Library of Success, you may find particularly useful content components in these sections: Comparisons, Downsides, Credibility, and Inspiration.

Your ideal outcome is to showcase your solution as superior. The ideal refrain in your audience's brain is: "Wow! Now I see why your solution is ideal!"

ACT TWO, SEGMENT THREE: IGNITE URGENCY

Segment Three is structured to create fear of missing out and inspire their desire to take action. For example, if they completed an assessment as part of Act Two, they might get the answers now. Those answers would fulfill your promise and get them anxious to take the next step.

Give them a reason to ask you how they can move forward. Portray a small window of opportunity. To heighten their desire, offer something special if they act while you are together. You might construct a limited time offer for a special price, high-value bundle, a small number of available seats, exclusive inventory, or the like. Hold off on giving the details about claiming it, unless they interrupt you because they are ready to take action. Otherwise, wait until your Great Closing to fully inform them about how to get it.

In the Library of Success, you may find particularly useful content components in these sections: Interactivity, Tips, and Accountability.

Your ideal outcome is to present an incentive to take the next step. The ideal refrain in your audience's brain is: "Wow! I don't want to make a mistake and miss out!"

ACT THREE: YOUR GREAT CLOSING

Now you leverage the transformation you engineered in Act One and Act Two. However, to ensure your success you first deepen the relationship and reinforce the messages you instilled. While this is your closing, it is not hard, pushy, or uncomfortable. It flows naturally because you already won their hearts and minds. They will be ready to do exactly what you planned.

Act Three, Segment One: Recall Promises Kept

Segment One is structured to remind your audience why they trust you, like you, and care about you. First, you recall the promise you made in Act One. Then, highlight the content that shows how you kept that promise in Act Two. For example, you might refer to a hands-on demonstration that gave them mastery over a new process as you promised. Avoid adding anything new at this point or going back through the details.

There is a simple formula for recalling the promises you kept. You complete this sentence, "When we first came together, I promised ..." Then, describe how your content in Act Two fulfilled the promise you made in Act One. If there remains an action to complete, let them know that is coming right up.

Your ideal outcome is to deepen the relationship. The ideal refrain in your audience's brain is: "Wow! You did exactly what you said you would!"

Act Three, Segment Two: Add Unexpected Value

Segment Two is structured to put the audience genuinely in your debt. You surprise them with a valuable add-on offer or unexpected benefit of taking the last action that fulfills your promise. For example, you might have an exclusive report, access to a free trial, or a contest with prizes. That may be a further incentive to take action when you give instructions in segment three.

The goal is to magnify their satisfaction with your presentation and you, so what they receive seems outsized compared to the time, attention, and involvement they gave you. This tips the "Relationship Scale" so the imbalance between what they got and what they gave is almost uncomfortable. That triggers the "Rule of Reciprocity," the natural urge to balance things out. You will give them that opportunity in Segment Three.

Your ideal outcome is to create "reciprocity anxiety." The ideal refrain in your audience's brain is: "Wow! You are over-delivering on your promises!"

Act Three, Segment Three:
Give Instructions and Get Action

Segment Three is structured to get the audience focused on doing exactly what you want them to do and how you want them to do it, which is the outcome you planned for this presentation. You respectfully give clear instructions for taking action. This action may be related to claiming the unexpected added value or completing the task that fulfills your promise. Then, you watch them follow your instructions.

Finally, you give instructions for any future commitments you want. For example, you may want to set up the next meeting or direct what they do as a follow-up to your presentation. Make sure to have everything you need to succeed: computer, calendar, pens, worksheets, URLs, and more. Then, acknowledge the excellent work or outcomes achieved, and say your farewells.

Your ideal outcome is to give instructions, get action, and secure future commitments. The ideal refrain in your audience's brain is: "Wow! I am moving forward on my goals!"

ONWARD TO EXAMPLES!

The next four chapters will show you the Speak Up System in action.

Section Three

The Speak Up System in Action

WHAT'S IN THIS SECTION?

Chapter 7: Persuasive Example

Chapter 8: Training Example

Chapter 9: Team Example

Chapter 10: Briefing Example

Section Three
Key Concepts

IN THIS SECTION, YOU SEE FOUR EXAMPLES USING THE SPEAK UP SYSTEM. Each example illustrates one of the four interaction styles that create specific transformations in your audience.

For more about each interaction style, turn to the Appendix: Helpful Resources. You will see how to choose the right style, so you swiftly achieve your goals for an audience, based on the type of resistance you anticipate before you craft your presentation. You will also discover how to customize your content for personality types (players) and even how to "orchestrate" your content by changing up the pitch, pace, and volume throughout your presentation. Plus, you'll find the Library of Success, to help you select the perfect content.

In the upcoming examples, notice how the SPEAK UP SYSTEM forms a reliable backbone of success, no matter what audience you have or what outcome you desire.

CHAPTER 7

Persuasive Presentation

Persuasive-style interactions can spark interest or motivate players who are indifferent or negative. You can transform their attitude into enthusiasm and positivity, so they take the actions you desire.

In this example, a volunteer makes a presentation to a group of lifelong learners who are committed to their own education but are disinclined to engage in community service. The speaker is an advocate for a non-profit that welcomes participation at all levels from people who can help make a difference in the lives of foster children.

The proximate outcome of the presentation is to get players to contact her directly so she can help them connect with one of several programs that could use their skills and interests.

The text under each title is a portion of one presentation,
with each section illustrating a specific element of THE SPEAK UP SYSTEM

EXAMPLE: PERSUASIVE-STYLE PRESENTATION
Topic: Good citizenship via volunteering
Audience: Lifelong learners in a communication skills course
Mindset Transformation: Indifferent to enthusiastic

ACT ONE: GREAT OPENING

GREAT OPENING, SEGMENT ONE: INTRODUCE YOURSELF
It was a day of contradictions. As I knocked on the door, on a gorgeous June day, the sun was shining. However, I was really nervous. I felt like Alice going through the looking glass. With that one knock on the door, I would cross over into a world so riddled with sadness and despair; anyone else would have cried or walked away. However, I was there on a rescue mission.

The door opened, and I saw her. A six-year-old little girl fidgeting on the couch with shy brown eyes and a smile, one of those pretend smiles that kids plaster on their little faces when they are afraid. Angela was one of five kids born to a drug-addicted mom. Just a few weeks before, I had been sworn in by a judge from Children's Court of Los Angeles as a Court Appointed Advocate. My name is Christy Tonette. From the time I was a young girl, I've worked with abused and neglected children sometimes as a paid employee, usually as a volunteer, but always as an advocate.

GREAT OPENING, SEGMENT TWO: INTRODUCE YOUR TOPIC
I know these children—I really know them. I've been at Children's Institute International, at their shelter that often first houses children after they've been removed from their homes. I've seen these kids run around like wild animals, just screaming. I've walked into a room full of toddlers, and before I can sit down, they're grabbing my legs wanting me to hold them. I've had children ask me if they could be my little girl or boy, and I've listened to a 3-year-old tell me how scary it was to be locked in a closet when his mom went out. I know these kids. They are foster children.

Great Opening, Segment Three: Make Promises

By the time we come to the end of our time together today, you'll be able to make an impact. Not just on these children, but on the soul of our society. You'll see how vital you can be to fostering our values and principles, not just children who have been cast aside. You will have an inroad into being a good citizen.

ACT TWO: STREAMLINED CONTENT

Streamlined Content, Segment One: Foster Understanding

How did foster care get started?

- In the 1600's there were no welfare programs. Authorities took abused, neglected or orphaned children and made them indentured servants to other families. They were "too useful to throw away."
- In the 1700's "vendoring" or a public auction gave the lowest bidder the right to take an orphan home in return for a weekly stipend paid by the town. The children provided additional labor.
- In the 1800s and 1900's children were often simply abandoned. The influx of immigrants to the United States surpassed many parents' ability to make a living. That poverty left children abandoned to live on their own. In 1854, it is estimated 34,000 homeless children were somehow subsisting, on their own in New York City.
- Early solutions to this wave of children without families to care for them, set the framework for the foster care system as it is today.
- The founder of the modern foster care movement is Charles Loring Brace who founded the Children's Aid Society. This organization sheltered children orphaned by communicable diseases like TB, cholera—and even alcohol abuse—that disabled or killed their parents living in crowded tenements. At the time, one thousand impoverished immigrants from rural America and Europe flooded NYC daily.
- Brace changed these children's future. They went from being indentured servants in cities to living with farm families where the children were to live for free but "serve as an extra pair of hands to help with the chores around the farm."

Thus the "Orphan Train" began. Children were gathered off the streets, taken out of jails and given over to Brace by their overburdened mothers in hopes that moving to the country would lead to a better life. Once the train arrived in a town, the children were lined up on stage for the audience to view them. One woman who rode the Orphan Train said it was a "strange feeling" to be on view like that and that it was "an ordeal that no child should go through" as she remembered a man "putting his tobacco-coated fingers in her mouth to check the quality of her teeth."

Nearly a century later, we flash forward to the amazing decade of the 1960's. Eighty-eight years after the first litigated case of child abuse in our nation, federal legislation on child abuse was passed as an amendment to the Social Security Act, revising the definition of child welfare services to include the prevention and remedy for child abuse.

Was it all solved then? Are children now protected or defended from abuse or abandonment? Unfortunately, there have not been significant advancements since 1854, concerning the quality of the foster care system.

- Statewide, only 132 full time and part time court officers are responsible for all the children in the system, creating an average caseload of 1,000 foster children per overseer.
- Attorneys caseloads average nearly three hundred children, and some attorneys handle 500 to 600 cases apiece. This far exceeds the recommended caseload of 188.
- At full capacity, Dodger stadium holds 56,000 people. In 2011, Los Angeles County had roughly the same number of children in foster care.

The Cost of Child Welfare:
- Foster children are likely to wind up without a high school education, graduating at about half the rate of children raised by their parents.
- Nationally, the U.S. spends more than $33 billion in direct costs resulting from abuse and neglect (costs related to immediate needs, such as child welfare and court services, hospitalization, mental health treatment, and law enforcement). We spend another $70 billion after foster care because the long-term results of abuse or neglect include special education, juvenile delinquency, adult criminality and lost productivity.

STREAMLINED CONTENT, SEGMENT TWO: CREATE BELIEF
The national Court Appointed Special Advocates Office (called CASA) has trained advocates, which is what I do. CASA has found that a child who has a volunteer advocate is more likely to:
- Find a safe, permanent home
- Get help while in the system
- Have a consistent, responsible adult presence
- Spend less time in foster care
- Avoid getting bounced from foster home to foster home
- Do better in school

In addition, CASA kids are evidencing 1) a more positive attitude towards the future, 2) the ability to work with others and manage conflict, 3) an increased sense of acceptance, 4) healthy behaviors and 5) better control over deviant behavior.

CASA is just one of many successful volunteer organizations making a difference in the lives of foster children.

STREAMLINED CONTENT, SEGMENT THREE: IGNITE URGENCY
As Andrew Carnegie stated, "Do real and permanent good in this world."

That's precisely what professionals or volunteers do, one person at a time. The philanthropists among us may choose to financially support an institution or fund the development of good orphanages. For the rest of us, there are very personal and effective ways to contribute to changing a child's life.

What can you do to improve a foster child's life on your own, starting tomorrow morning? You can make a phone call and volunteer to use your hobbies or skills to improve the lives of these children and improve how they impact our society. You can act on your personal values and create a legacy that lives on in others.

Two good places to start are by calling Hillsides Home for Children, and Court Appointed Advocates Office. You might recruit a friend or loved one to make this commitment together.

For example, you might offer to:
- Teach a basic cooking class
- Tutor kids in a school subject, like math or reading skills
- Provide support for learning computer programs like Word or Excel

- Hold a short seminar on dressing for job interviews
- Teach a class on how to set up a bank account and handle a debit card
- Perhaps you have a business where you could provide employment
- Also, maybe you could raise funds among your family and friends for a program you start or one that exists

Carl Sagan said, "We're made of star stuff." I say, you and I just need to shine some light or give some attention to these kids at a time in their lives when a good deed will pay a lifetime of dividends.

Are you ready to shine a little of your light where otherwise there is darkness and despair?

ACT THREE: GREAT CLOSING

Great Closing, Segment One: Recall Promises Kept

When we first came together today, I promised I'd show you how you would be able to make an impact. Not just on these children, but on the soul of our society. You see how vital you can be to fostering our values and principles, not just children who have been cast aside. You have a new inroad into how to be a good citizen.

You've heard the statistics and stories, and you have an idea of the help that's needed, and some ideas about how you can provide that help.

Great Closing, Segment Two: Add Unexpected Value

What I didn't tell you about is the real benefit, the actual thrill of working with foster children whose lives are transformed by your guidance. Imagine watching their successes as I have. Let me come to a close with several examples. That little girl I told you about when we started? After four years in foster care and five placements, that child was adopted into a good home and is thriving. I know this because I get a Christmas card from her every year.

There's a program called The Youth Moving On program at Hillsides Home for Children to help emancipating youth, those who are 18 and leave the foster care system.

I don't know who funded it, but it started with one person's idea. Recently, five kids who aged out of the system traveled to Le Blanc, France. There they studied with tradespeople who are experts in 17th-century carpentry and modern-day landscaping. When the kids returned home, they created the most beautiful planters for Hillsides. At this same facility, several youths started a clothing line called Indigenous Peeples.

Everything that made these kids' lives better started as an idea, which was followed by action. That's how the CASA program that advocates for children in foster care started.

GREAT CLOSING, SEGMENT THREE:
GIVE INSTRUCTIONS AND GET ACTION

Susan B. Anthony stated, "Organize, agitate, educate must be our cry."

Would you right now, write down one skill you have that you could use to educate a foster child? Something that comes easily to you. Maybe it's a hobby you enjoy. A language you know. Or a subject you could tutor a child in school, or something you could do for a child about to become 18 who will be looking for a job.

Let's take just 15 seconds and write down the first thing that comes to mind. Now I'd like to go around the room and have us each share just one thing each that we could do to improve a foster child's life. I'll go first. I can share my love for crafting by teaching kids how to yarn paint.

What can you do? (*facilitates audience participation*)

I'm going to leave you with my email so that if you like, I can help you connect with a program that will so appreciate your interest in helping.

I'll close my presentation with these words from two foster children who made a big impression on my heart. Stephanie age nine in foster care said it best. She declared: "I will be proud when I grow up. I will be a hero." Also, Susanna age ten shared words I hope you remember in her honor. She said, "I am a foster kid, and I am good. Do not forget Susanna."

Section Three
CHAPTER 8

Training Presentation

T RAINING-STYLE INTERACTIONS ARE IDEAL WHEN YOUR AUDIENCE
lacks the skills or knowledge to take action as you desire. You transform
that deficit into proficiency and confidence. Training might be the
actual end goal, such as learning a new software program. However, sales
representatives often use training-style presentations when the underlying
resistance to their solution is the audience's ignorance or their fear it will be
too difficult to implement.

In this example, a job candidate speaks to manufacturers about hiring her,
even though she does not have direct experience.

Her proximate outcome is to get manufacturers signed up for a free
consultation, as a trial before employing her.

*The text under each title is a portion of one presentation,
with each section illustrating a specific element of* THE SPEAK UP SYSTEM

EXAMPLE: TRAINING-STYLE PRESENTATION

Topic: How to hire the ideal remotely located employee

Audience: Distributors hiring workers abroad

Mindset Transformation: Uncertain to confident

ACT ONE: GREAT OPENING

GREAT OPENING, SEGMENT ONE: INTRODUCE YOURSELF

Thirty years ago my parents moved from China to Spain and opened one of the first Chinese restaurants in Barcelona, where I was born. Because their priority was working to survive, they didn't have time and energy to dedicate to learn Spanish. So, from a very young age, I became not only my parents' translator but also their interpreter. It was frustrating, uncomfortable, and even overwhelming going to the bank, on shopping trips, and especially to the doctor. However, I had to be there because my parents relied on me. That was the least I could do to repay all their sacrifices.

Hi, I'm Maya Cheng, an international business consultant fluent in five languages. I understand how cultural differences affect negotiations. My job is to provide information, assess weaknesses, and not stop until I find the right solutions for companies doing business overseas.

GREAT OPENING, SEGMENT TWO: INTRODUCE YOUR TOPIC

That mentality is what brought me to the US five years ago to pursue a career in international business. By that time I had met the love of my life and started a long distance relationship. Falling in love is not the same as staying in love. Falling in love was the easy part. To stay in love especially living five thousand miles apart, we had to deal with challenges like trust issues, time management, and constant open communication. Love didn't happen to us. We are in love because we both chose to be.

Every day I make the choice to love someone without knowing he will choose to love me, too. And that is terrifying. The same situation happens in business.

Every day you have the chance to decide to retain someone without knowing he would be as committed as you are to achieving your company's goals.

In business, like in love, we want to find the perfect long-term partner, a person we can trust, share and connect with, because even if we are ten miles apart, every day is a challenge. So, how do you decide who deserves your commitment?

Great Opening, Segment Three: Make Promises

I promise, by the end of our time together, you will be able to look at people like myself who survived and enjoyed a long-distance relationship in a different way. Like a company such as Coca-Cola or Unilever that operates by empowering partners in many different markets, you will discover qualities like trust, perseverance, and commitment. Traits that maybe you don't have in your team at headquarters right now, but with a remote distributor you will need to increase productivity and decrease personnel costs.

ACT TWO: STREAMLINED CONTENT

Streamlined Content, Segment One: Foster Understanding

There are 14 million people only in the US who define themselves as having a long distance relationship, and this number is increasing with the introduction of new technologies. On average, most people tend to be 125 miles apart, visit each other twice a month and call every three days. Of course, not all long distance relationships survive, 40% of them end with a breakup. That means 60% of them succeed if they frequently communicate, commit to mutual goals, and trust each other.

Still, long-distance couples must make an effort when they want the relationship to last. Not taking the time to plan for successful communication is the most common cause of failure.

In the workplace, a study found that between 50 to 70% of change initiatives fail. Many common reasons for this failure are time management, unclear communication, and lack of planning. All the qualities that people in long-distance relationships have developed to thrive.

STREAMLINED CONTENT, SEGMENT TWO: CREATE BELIEF

I know you can hire someone already entrenched in the retail, wholesale and distribution industry, but industry needs are changing every day. You need someone who is familiar with the use of new technologies to accelerate operations while reducing logistics costs. Someone who can do this remotely, in a trustworthy manner.

On the other hand, you can hire someone who only speaks Chinese, because the majority of your suppliers are in that region. However, that would only cover your surface deficits. In the long term, you would like to expand to other countries, and a Chinese speaker won't be able to communicate with all your valuable prospects and clients.

Lastly, you can hire someone who has survived and enjoyed a long distance relationship and understands the challenges of working overseas leading people from different backgrounds. Someone who communicates effectively, who is comfortable planning, and has a proven record making and keeping long-term commitments. That will give you a jump on productivity while decreasing personnel costs.

I wanted to show you alternatives, provide fresh air for your thinking, and share the skills I internalized through my years of experience in a long-term relationship. This experience translates into business skills I would apply to achieve your company goals.

STREAMLINED CONTENT, SEGMENT THREE: IGNITE URGENCY

Well-known companies in the industry like Procter and Gamble are already looking for people with these three qualities: commitment, trust, and perseverance to work toward their long-term goals. I've allotted two months to land in this position and bring these qualities to a consumer goods distributor company. In my previous job, I negotiated ocean transportations in Chinese, English, and Spanish to reduce freight costs while increasing sales by 20%. I don't know if I can do the same for you, but I would love you to experience what it's like to work with me, a trustworthy committed distributor. You don't want to lose me to a competitor and miss out!

ACT THREE: GREAT CLOSING

Great Closing, Segment One: Recall Promises Kept

At the beginning of this meeting, I promised you would be able to look at people in long-distance relationships from a different perspective, as trustworthy and committed employees. The success stories and the skills to thrive can all be applied in the workplace. I also promised you would be able to choose these qualities over more basic experience to fulfill the needs of your company, to increase productivity and decrease personnel costs.

Great Closing, Segment Two: Add Unexpected Value

Now, I'd like to offer you a little something from me to you. You'll receive a 90-minute consulting "date" with me, so you can immediately see how I put into practice all my skills.

Great Closing, Segment Three:
Give Instructions and Get Action

This consulting time is typically $150, but it is yours for free if you write down your phone number here. Don't worry, this is a business "date." So, I'll call you back! Just write your phone number here, and you can count on me to call you back this week. It is a pleasure to make your acquaintance.

Section Three
CHAPTER 9

Team Presentation

T EAM-STYLE INTERACTIONS ARE IDEAL WHEN INDIVIDUALS ARE SELF-
centered or disconnected from each other. You transform their fractured
interests into a unified desire to reach a group goal. This is the right style
for launching a new initiative or aligning the interests of different departments.

In this example, an event coordinator speaks with employees and contractors
who must work together on a strict budget to produce a festival. She knows
some of the players but must also introduce first time participants to the project.

Her proximate outcome is to set up one-on-one meetings so each team
member can commit to a plan of action that leads to achieving the group's goal.

The text under each title is a portion of one presentation,
with each section illustrating a specific element of The Speak Up System

---

EXAMPLE: TEAM-STYLE PRESENTATION

Topic: Planning an event on a tight budget

Audience: Employees and contractors

Mindset Transformation: Self-centered to group goal-oriented

ACT ONE: GREAT OPENING

GREAT OPENING, SEGMENT ONE: INTRODUCE YOURSELF

As Sam Ewig once said: Hard work spotlights the character of people. Some turn up their sleeves, some turn up their noses, and some don't turn up at all. Hi, I am Judith Wyatt, your team leader and Skystream Studio's employee number three—which means I used to work for the free lunch here because that's all we got "paid" back then!

As is Sam's credo and our company's work ethic: Let's ensure we are the ones who turn up our sleeves, dive in, and show results.

GREAT OPENING, SEGMENT TWO: INTRODUCE YOUR TOPIC

The upcoming company event has three primary goals we need to achieve to stay on top of our game and exceed the praise we received in the previous year.

1. We need to stay within our budget,
2. International delegate numbers have increased from last year, so we must make sure enough seats in theaters are available at the various screenings plus food and transportation are sufficient, and
3. Security is vital for all screenings as we want to ensure that filmmakers can trust us.

That is why we are here today: to implement and improve procedures, tighten the schedule, and perfect the communication among our team. While we are running around like crazy people, let's do it with smiles and grace!

Great Opening, Segment Three: Make Promises

I promise that this meeting will be worth your time and at the end of this meeting you will leave with a clear picture of what your desired outcome will be from this project. You will see where you can mature within your area of responsibility. I also promise that once we revise the event schedule and strategic work plan, you will be able to voice any concerns and bring suggestions to the table to make this event indeed a team effort and run as smoothly as possible.

ACT TWO: STREAMLINED CONTENT

Streamlined Content, Segment One: Foster Understanding

In the hand-outs I provided you with at the beginning of the meeting, you will find rough drafts of both the festival schedule and the strategic work schedule. You can see most of the ownership blocks associated with assignments are left blank. I would like you to consider what assignments would leverage the highest and best use of your talent. Also, I would like you to think about what you would like to learn, perhaps as the second in charge so you can assist someone who can show you the ropes.

We plan to meet each week when we each report progress, challenges, or forecasts of what might fall through the cracks.

We are here to support each other so be sure to raise your hand when you need help. Be alert to when you can help out a teammate or call something to their attention.

Streamlined Content, Segment Two: Create Belief

Keep in mind, that trying to take on too much responsibility by one's self is a common occurrence when putting together meetings and events of such caliber. Therefore, I suggest we each take on only as much as we can handle. We need to empower ourselves through each team member's strengths. If we amplify each individual's contribution and we look out for each other during the planning and implementation, we can be creative and effective in solving any potential problems ahead of time.

Being proactive in your work and aware of how team members are doing will enrich your overall experience of this event and help accomplish expected goals from our superiors as a team.

STREAMLINED CONTENT, SEGMENT THREE: IGNITE URGENCY
With so much information and knowledge shared with you so far in our meeting, take it all in for a moment and process it.

Now, let me take you through the week's events on the schedule, and also the strategic work document to guide you through the thought process behind them. Please carefully consider what I am sharing to see how we can increase productivity and possibly look at some cost savings by analyzing venues and headcount. (*Judith takes the team through documents and invites questions and answers.*)

ACT THREE: GREAT CLOSING

GREAT CLOSING, SEGMENT ONE: RECALL PROMISES KEPT
This morning, I kicked off the meeting with two promises. First promise: you will leave this meeting with a clear picture of what this project entails and what your areas of duties and responsibilities will be. In our questions and answers session, we have been able to get volunteers for almost everything on our lists.

Second promise: that once we revised the event schedule and strategic work plan, you would be able to voice any concerns and bring suggestions to the table to make this event a team effort and run as smoothly as possible. Once again, our questions and answers session did a great job of raising and addressing so many. I invite you to continue doing such a great job at each weekly meeting!

GREAT CLOSING, SEGMENT TWO: ADD UNEXPECTED VALUE
Now, I'd like to offer you a little something from me to you. In recognition of the hard work our team will put into this project, I would like to offer all of us a wine tasting trip up to Santa Barbara upon completion of this project. We will leave on a Monday morning and come back Wednesday evening. I will research some lovely chateaus that are available for us all to stay in and come back to you with some recommendations so we can then make a united decision. This gift is a token of my appreciation of your hard work!

GREAT CLOSING, SEGMENT 3:
GIVE INSTRUCTIONS AND GET ACTION
However, before we taste the wine on our palates, here is what I would like you to do next. Please be sure to take your copies of the event schedule and work

plan with you. Go back to your office and familiarize yourself with these. Then, I would like each of you to work on your respective duties and responsibilities over the next two days and schedule individual meetings with me for us to go over your sections and discuss your tactics and strategies.

Now let's get this show quite literally on the road!

Briefing Presentation

A BRIEFING-STYLE PRESENTATION IS IDEAL WHEN YOUR AUDIENCE SEEMS "stuck" or has limited information that holds them back from taking action. You transform that mindset so they are fully updated and proactive. This is the right style to energize an audience to take action.

In this example, an entrepreneur introduces his website, which helps sports team managers do a better job of managing their team schedules and communicating with teammates. While they each have a way of doing that now, he wants to improve their results by showing them an updated approach that saves time.

His proximate outcome is getting them signed up to use a free trial of his software, which will lead to their purchase of his system.

The text under each title is a portion of one presentation,
with each section illustrating a specific element of THE SPEAK UP SYSTEM

EXAMPLE: BRIEFING-STYLE PRESENTATION
Topic: Managing a sports team
Audience: Local sports team coaches
Mindset Transformation: Stuck to proactive
Note: Website mentioned is not the actual site

ACT ONE: GREAT OPENING

Great Opening, Segment One: Introduce Yourself

According to a recent poll conducted by Harris Interactive, Americans spend an average of 46 hours per week working. Factoring in additional time spent commuting, housekeeping, studying, sleeping and other commitments, the same survey revealed that Americans have just 16 hours to play per week. That's down by 20% from the results of the same poll conducted in 2007. Hi, I'm Bill Chatham, founder of SportsTeamManager.com. Please think of us as people working to extend recess.

Great Opening, Segment Two: Introduce Your Topic

I started my own basketball league out of college and tracked player statistics just as a way to stay connected with friends and exercise competitively. However, I soon learned how cumbersome the administrative side of managing a sports league could be. I realized I was spending most of my time inefficiently: sifting through long email chains just to set up schedules, manually recording player statistics and then transferring that information to my computer, and updating the league website by editing HTML code after each game.

Accordingly, I looked towards products in the marketplace that would help me reduce the time spent performing these tasks so that I could spend more time enjoying what I wanted to all along: playing basketball and spending time with my friends. However, most of these products were either outdated, overly complicated or did not address my needs. My frustration led me to take action. I teamed up with my business partner and together drawing upon our expertise in web application development, we built a better sports management application which I am going to share with you today.

Great Opening, Segment Three: Make Promises

By the end of our time together, I guarantee you will experience the most simple, versatile, and efficient way to manage an amateur sports team. I promise our web application will save you time and the frustration of the administrative duties.

ACT TWO: STREAMLINED CONTENT

Streamlined Content, Segment One: Foster Understanding

Simply stated, SportsTeamManager.com is a convenient way to manage your sports team online. In literally seconds, you can create an account on our website. Then you'll have access to a wide range of useful coaching tools including scheduling, statistics record-keeping, and team communication across a full spectrum of sports: from the most popular—baseball, basketball, football, and soccer—to bowling, darts, and even ultimate Frisbee.

Streamlined Content, Segment Two: Create Belief

Many sports team coaches in your area have already taken advantage of our product and have discovered how helpful our tools really are. You'll find a list of teams with testimonials from both coaches and players plus a complete list of sports we cover in the information packet you'll get at the end of our time together.

While developing our product, we talked to dozens of coaches like you. We learned one common trait all of them wanted in their sports management software. Our product provides that one thing our competitors don't—simplicity. Our dynamic web application provides you with an easy and intuitive way to input your player stats that will save you time. Plus, you get an organized way to communicate with players and parents so you'll never be involved in one of those annoying email chains ever again, and user-controlled privacy settings so you can feel secure about who has access to your team's information.

Streamlined Content, Segment Three: Ignite Urgency

Furthermore, we offer fixed pricing plans starting at just $4.95/month for the whole team. You can expect to pay four times that amount using other sports management software out there that charge fees based on the number of players. And good luck trying to figure out how they arrived at their prices! These are just a few ways we take the hassle out of managing your team. But don't take our word for it, next we will be going into a quick demonstration of our product.

[Product demonstration setting up a test account tailored to coach]

As you can see, you can now save yourself so much time and the frustration that comes along with managing your sports team. I also want you to understand that we are always here to help you. Not only can you call our toll-free customer support number with any questions or concerns about our product, but when you sign up today, I will also give you my personal contact information before our time together is over so you can reach me with any questions or concerns that you'd like for me to address personally.

ACT THREE: GREAT CLOSING

Great Closing, Segment One: Recall Promises Kept

I promised when we began today that you'd be exposed to the most simple, versatile, and efficient way to manage your sports teams. I said that our product would do two things for you: 1) significantly reduce the administrative time you spend managing your team, and 2) minimize the frustration of coaching administration. Today you have seen exactly how.

Great Closing, Segment Two: Add Unexpected Value

I want you to realize not only are we invested in making your life easier as a coach, but we are also invested in your success. So, I am happy to give you a 2-week risk-free trial on the test account we created for you today so that you can try it out for yourself on your own time. In addition, I would like you to have this book on effective coaching from one of the greatest sports coaches in history—John Wooden. The book reveals Wooden's coaching philosophy that helped him get the best out of his players and won him 10 NCAA national championships.

In the same way, I have found success in applying his philosophy to managing my own basketball league; I'm sure you will find much value in incorporating his knowledge into your own way of coaching. Would you like that?

GREAT CLOSING, SEGMENT 3:
GIVE INSTRUCTIONS AND GET ACTION

Simply go to our website, www.SportsTeamManager.com and log in using your trial account username and password that you created during the product demo today. At the end of the two-week trial, we'll send you Coach Wooden's book along with the option of extending your service at our low monthly rate.

Once again, just log in to SportsTeamManager.com. Use your free trial for two weeks. And, if you love the experience, you get the option of extending your service at the low monthly rate and enjoy your copy of Coach Wooden's book.

Here's to enjoying the pleasures of coaching, with more gain and less pain! ◼

The Speak Up System

Section Four

Act 1, Segment 1 (Introduce Yourself)

WHAT'S IN THIS SECTION?

Chapter 11: Your Heroic Achievement Story

Chapter 12: Your Startling Statistic

Chapter 13: Your Dramatic Quotation

ACT 1: GREAT OPENING
  Segment 1: Introduce Yourself
  Segment 2: Introduce Topic
  Segment 3: Make Promises
ACT 2: STREAMLINED CONTENT
  Segment 1: Foster Understanding
  Segment 2: Create Belief
  Segment 3: Ignite Urgency
ACT 3: GREAT CLOSING
  Segment 1: Recall Promises Kept
  Segment 2: Add Unexpected Value
  Segment 3: Give Instructions

Section Four
Key Concepts

THIS SECTION EXPLORES THE ALTERNATIVE WAYS TO INTRODUCE YOURSELF, which takes place in the first segment of your Great Opening in the SPEAK UP SYSTEM. Introducing yourself is a crucial step in getting your audience to trust you, like you, and care about you. Plus, you must get their attention.

Your ideal outcome is this refrain in your audience's brain: "Wow, you have remarkable experience, I feel lucky to listen to you!"

What's the difference between the alternatives? A heroic achievement story is great for showcasing your values and character. A startling statistic is a fast way to share an achievement. A dramatic quotation conveys your philosophy or motivation.

There is a chapter for each style of introducing yourself, with formulas and examples. For each presentation you make, choose just one of the alternatives.

Section Four
CHAPTER 11

Heroic Achievement

Alternative #1 for a Great Opening, Segment One (Introduce Yourself)

THE FIRST ALTERNATIVE FOR INTRODUCING YOURSELF IS THE HEROIC Achievement story, which is perfect when you want to highlight your values or qualities. It's the most powerful way to influence or reframe an audience's perception of you. When they might underestimate the utility of your experience, education, or background, this is the ideal way to introduce yourself.

BE DRAMATIC

The best way to introduce yourself to an audience is through a dramatic account of an accomplishment or result you achieved in the face of significant odds. That's the basis of your heroic achievement story. Engage your audience and inspire confidence as you share the salient details of solving a problem they can relate to. Make sure to highlight which of your personal qualities were critical in your achieving results.

Stories teach, they don't preach. Even better, stories remain in the brain. Long after you've left your audience, your story will live on in their minds. That's key to getting the commitments you need from an audience and getting those commitments to stick.

TIPS FOR A MEMORABLE HEROIC ACHIEVEMENT STORY
- Tell the story in chronological order.
- Set the scene. Describe the setting and what specifically made the situation or conditions difficult for you, your company, or a client.
- Add details about the problems. What particular risks or consequences did you have to confront?

TIPS AND TACTICS

Explain how you resolved the situation. Make sure you reference how you did it, not just that you got it done. What solution did you use, invent, create, or select? Then, describe the excellent result, as well as how you achieved it as quickly as possible and at the smallest possible expense.

Then tell the audience your name and job title or the focus of your work, if they don't already know that.

Highlight a key benefit or quality that makes you and your story universally appealing. Since heroic achievement stories are about specific events, this last sentence is meant to telegraph the greater meaning at the heart of your story.

Your heroic achievement story does not have to be directly related to the industry or specific problem your audience is facing. Remember, this segment introduces YOU as a human being—so choose a story that demonstrates your personal qualities or your values. Your ideal outcome is to help the audience see you as a unique, valuable, and one-of-a-kind individual who brings your personal best to any situation. Highlight your best character traits in action.

GUIDELINES FOR A GREAT STORY
- Be brief
- Be bold
- Be brilliant

FORMULA FOR YOUR HEROIC ACHIEVEMENT STORY
1. Set the scene and reveal the conditions.
2. Create conflict using action words—build suspense.
3. Resolve the conflict with maximum effectiveness and minimum cost.
4. Formally introduce the hero (you) and broadcast the moral.

EXAMPLE #1

"Off the coast of Singapore on a sweltering August morning, I stood waist high in a well of crude oil and sand, waiting for our company's helicopter to drop the one part that would get our client's plant up and running. By midday, we installed the part, and the client was in operation. We actually retrofitted our device into a competitor's system on the spot to minimize cost and downtime. All this happened within 24 hours of their call for help. I'm Jim Mariz, a sales representative for Gergen Oil Tools. My job is to do what it takes to keep our clients' production up."

Let's take that example step by step

Step 1: *Set the scene and reveal the conditions*
"Off the coast of Singapore on a sweltering August morning,"

Step 2: *Create conflict using action words—build suspense*
"I stood waist high in a well of crude oil and sand, waiting for our company's helicopter to drop the one part that would get our client's plant up and running."

Step 3: *Resolve the conflict with maximum effectiveness, minimum cost*
"By midday, we installed the part, and the client was in operation. We actually retrofitted our device into a competitor's system on the spot to minimize cost and downtime. All this happened within 24 hours of their call for help."

Step 4: *Formally introduce the hero (you) and broadcast the moral*
"I'm Jim Mariz, a sales representative for Gergen Oil Tools. My job is to do what it takes to keep our clients' production up."

EXAMPLE #2:

"During a firestorm of activity in IT after the first bank of servers went down, I got a line into our CFO's office just four minutes before the investor conference call was set to begin. I briefed him on the most crucial details: the extent of the blackout, the effect on our users, and the best estimate of when we would be fully operational. I'm Jennifer Lipton, a 10 year veteran here. Our department's open communication with top management is proof that our company's mission statement really means something."

Let's take that example step by step

Step 1: *Set the scene and reveal the conditions*
"During a firestorm of activity in IT after the first bank of servers went down,"

Step 2: *Create conflict using action words—build suspense*
"I got a line into our CFO's office just four minutes before the investor conference call was set to begin."

Step 3: *Resolve the conflict with maximum effectiveness, minimum cost*
"I briefed him on the most crucial details: the extent of the blackout, the effect on our users, and the best estimate of when we would be fully operational."

Step 4: *Formally introduce the hero (you) and broadcast the moral*
"I'm Jennifer Lipton, a 10 year veteran here. Our department's open communication with top management is proof that our company's mission statement really means something."

ONWARD!

In the next chapter, we look at an alternative way to introduce yourself, using a startling statistic.

Section Four
CHAPTER 12

Startling Statistics

Alternative #2 for a Great Opening, Segment One (Introduce Yourself)

T HE SECOND ALTERNATIVE FOR INTRODUCING YOURSELF IS THE Startling Statistic, which is perfect when you are short on time, or your audience is disengaged. Evoke immediate "shock and awe" by emphasizing the metrics of a specific achievement. Tie that performance to a personal quality such as your inventiveness or honesty to showcase what drove the extraordinary results.

THERE'S POWER IN NUMBERS

Startling statistics are a fast-acting alternative when compared to heroic achievement stories. Surprise your audience, awakening them to not just what you do but why you do it. This is ideal when you are presenting to an audience that's familiar with you, and you want to restructure or recalibrate what they think about you. In that case, give your statistic but leave out your name.

Startling statistics also make a great standalone introduction when you are at a networking event or a meeting where each person gets 15 seconds to introduce themselves. It's also a great way to introduce yourself in an elevator pitch or even when you bump into your new boss in the breakroom. Of course, it's a compelling way to launch your Great Opening in a presentation.

THERE'S VALUE IN VALUES

Why do numbers instantly inspire confidence? They are simple to communicate, yet easily represent impressive accomplishments. They show your priorities and therefore, telegraph your values. In the examples, you will see how statistics can communicate empowerment, security, vitality, creativity, and individuality.

FORMULA FOR A STARTLING STATISTIC
1. State an accomplishment, highlighting a metric such as a number, percentage, quantity, amount of money, or ratio.
2. Say your name and your title or function.
3. Connect your accomplishment to a value or larger lesson your audience will appreciate.

SHOWCASE YOUR VALUES WITH STARTLING STATISTICS
Here are some examples linked to values that may spark your own startling statistics.

Ambition
"I helped our department exceed its productivity goals for three consecutive years. Hi, I'm Mark Nelson, always focused on measurable improvement."

Security
"I created a backup system that automatically mirrored our data in a remote location instantly, 24/7/365. Hello, I am Liz Ng, a security-minded IT manager who loves delivering peace of mind."

Vitality
"I reinvigorated our brand by adding 15 new distribution points every quarter. Hi, I'm Francoise Nadal, totally committed to smart ways marketing can serve management's growth goals."

Creativity
"Our shareholders received the first interactive annual report, which became a model for our industry. Hi, I'm Rebecca Rocket, making documents come alive with the tricks of digital graphic design."

Individuality
"I authored the backgrounder for our CEO prior to his announcing the acquisition. He is highly visual, so I used three charts that captured over 100 data points for him. Hello, I'm Jet Torerk. When I understand how you think, I create reports that speak to you."

USE STARTLING STATISTICS FOR ANY INTERACTION STYLE

Below, you'll find examples for each of the four interaction styles—persuasive, team, training, and briefing. All three segments of the Great Opening are included to help you see how a startling statistic fits into a complete Act One in the SPEAK UP SYSTEM.

EXAMPLE: TRAINING SEMINAR

Situation/audience: My workshop on creating career transitions for mid-level managers.
Value: Vitality

SEGMENT ONE: INTRODUCE YOURSELF

"After 30 years in business, I'm enjoying my third major career change and planning my fourth! I'm Nance Rosen, the first woman director of marketing in the Global 2000 technology sector, youngest-ever general manager of a top-five ad agency and former host of International Business on public radio."

SEGMENT TWO: INTRODUCE YOUR TOPIC

"Have you ever wondered what it takes to make it to the top of your industry or profession and then jump off that platform to start something entirely new? Today you'll discover two career strategies. The first one accelerates your success in the company or industry you're in today. The second strategy builds on your current momentum by giving you the freedom to express your interests and talent. I'll prove that from where you are right now, you can take a giant leap forward toward your next career or even opening your own successful business."

SEGMENT THREE: MAKE PROMISES

"I promise by the end of our meeting today, you'll be able to create your very own 'Personalized Portfolio of Careers.' You'll have a plan for getting the maximum return on the most important investment you'll ever make: dedication to yourself. Are you ready?"

EXAMPLE: MANAGEMENT BRIEFING

Situation/audience: Amos Garcia briefs the new owners who recently acquired his company.
Value: Security

Segment One: Introduce Yourself

"Our manufacturing department has a perfect safety record for the longest stretch of time in the history of this company. Most of you know me, Amos Garcia, as the safety officer for Kligborne. Now my new title and one I worked hard to earn is your Director of Risk Management."

Segment Two: Introduce Your Topic

"To keep this amazing streak alive, a modest investment of $2,300 in equipment upgrades would be to our benefit. The company will see real cost savings by: 1) lowering our worker's compensation claims and expenses by 20%, and 2) lowering by half or entirely eliminating our costs for per diem or temporary workers. In the next ten minutes, I'm going to brief you on the equipment and training options. Then, I'll make a recommendation for the solution other companies have found to be successful under similar circumstances to ours."

Segment Three: Make Promises

"After this short visit, I guarantee you will have all the documentation you need to evaluate this purchase of upgrades. You'll be able to make the decision that best suits your plan for this department and our organization."

EXAMPLE: TEAM MEETING
Situation/audience: Emily Lau shares social media strategies with aspiring influencers.
Values: Creativity and Security

Segment One: Introduce Yourself

"As a social media micro-influencer, I designed engaging content that has attracted 20,000 followers so far. My strategy for long-term success is to continue building a family-friendly reputation in esports. Hello, I am Emily Lau, an ardent gamer, self-taught photographer, and brunch-loving Millennial."

Segment Two: Introduce Your Topic

"Can you have it all? Can you have it all at once? How much do you have to sacrifice your real life when you earn your living on social media? These are the sometimes painful questions I have answered in my own life. I want to help you answer the same questions and make a choice to live life on your own terms."

SEGMENT THREE: MAKE PROMISES

"By the end of our time together today, you will have not only my personal roadmap from obscurity to sponsored social media influencer. You will have your own plan for attracting followers who are seeking out the content you want to create."

EXAMPLE: PERSUASIVE PRESENTATION
Situation/audience: Brenton DeLeon sells components to a prospect.
Values: Empowerment and Vitality

SEGMENT ONE: INTRODUCE YOURSELF

"Until last month, I sold components on an exclusive basis to your company's largest competitor, which is also the industry's number one market leader. I'm Brenton DeLeon of Genisfare, Ltd."

SEGMENT TWO: INTRODUCE YOUR TOPIC

"I can make these components available to your company with the slight modifications you require, and that will be necessary, given my agreement with your competition. Until now, that would have been impossible. However with the launch of the new models, we have freedom from that absolute exclusivity."

SEGMENT THREE: MAKE PROMISES

"In our meeting today, I assure you that you'll have a plan to achieve the performance and sales results you desire. Plus, you will find our terms make it possible for you to buy components in the quantity you need and have them arrive just in time, to keep your production line optimized."

ONWARD!
Now let's progress to the last alternative for introducing yourself: the dramatic quotation.

Section Four
CHAPTER 13

Dramatic Quotation

Alternative #3 for a Great Opening, Segment One (Introduce Yourself)

T HE THIRD ALTERNATIVE FOR INTRODUCING YOURSELF IS A DRAMATIC Quotation, which is a perfect way to telegraph your philosophy, inspiration, or motivation. When you quote a thought-leader, you get a "halo effect." Plus, you showcase how literate you are. Alternatively, you may author a quote to highlight how your values inform your point of view.

COMMUNICATE YOUR PHILOSOPHY

Dramatic quotations get you the right kind of attention, especially when you intend to project a new image to an audience familiar with you. The quote you choose reveals something positive about your character. You want to select a quotation, or author one of your own, to show your unique perspective and values. It should also hint at how you will approach the concerns and problems of your audience.

This style of introducing yourself is compelling when your audience thinks they know you so well; you could not surprise them. Often, players have "pigeon-holed" you over time, assuming you are a person who always thinks a certain way, has command over only a limited amount of information, or might be underqualified for something you aspire to do now.

If you have changed, or you're about to change, how are you going to improve your reputation with others? Re-introducing yourself with a quotation is like borrowing the qualities, personal brand, or status of the person you are quoting! That can create a pretty dramatic transformation in an audience's perspective about you.

So, choose wisely. Remember, the quotation is meant to immediately inspire confidence, no matter how well your audience thinks they know you.

DRAMATIC QUOTATIONS TIPS

- A famous quotation is an excellent way to impress your audiences with the depth of your intelligence, authentic values, and breadth of interests.
- Select a quote that represents skills or attitudes that matter to your audience, such as ingenuity, dedication, or caring. You're telegraphing your mindset, specifically how you will approach your audience's needs or problems.
- Consider creating your own pithy quotation to surprise and impress your audience when they realize you are the author.

SHOWCASE YOUR VALUES

You might have a quotation that links you with a philosophy. Alternatively, select a sentiment that brings to mind a quality such as attention to detail, poise under pressure, or tenacity. Of course, the quotation might in some way reflect your experience, professional competence, training, unique skill, or attitude.

Although it's very brief, a quotation approximates the result you get from sharing a heroic achievement story. A quote may be less memorable than a heroic achievement because it is much briefer and lacks details. However, it's an excellent choice when you want to reveal something new about your character or perspective.

A dramatic quotation may be the words of a famous or revered person. Using a famous quote shows you have a depth of literacy, education, or worldliness that may surprise your audience. Just make sure that if you quote another person, you give them credit and do the best you can to mirror the intention of their sentiment.

Quoting a famous individual is easy. Just use a search engine and type in the value you want to communicate and the word quotation. That quotation helps you deliver a perfectly polished opening. However, you'll be especially impressive if you craft your own quote. Typically, your audience is delighted and surprised when you reveal you are the author.

In the following examples, you'll find information on the interaction style and the speaker's desired outcome. These details will help you see why the dramatic quotation was selected and why it was effective.

EXAMPLE: TRAINING SEMINAR

Audience/outcome: I help engineers and sales representatives transition to marketing roles.

"If your company were a horse, marketing would be the horse's nose. And, as the nose goes, so goes the whole horse. Marketers are trained to see what's happening on the road ahead. We influence the direction of an organization by communicating new information and our analysis of it. Our proactivity affects other departments, so they can correctly allocate resources, products, and people or acquire what they need to succeed. I'm Nance Rosen, happy to be your guide to the horsepower of professional marketing."

EXAMPLE: MANAGEMENT BRIEFING
Audience/outcome: A UX designer updates management on dangers lurking in the current IT platform.

"There's an African saying that's appropriate for us to meditate on right now. 'Better a mistake at the beginning than at the end.' As you know, I'm Roxanne Upton, and up until now, you haven't heard from me about IT, just design. However, given our new project, I want to tell you about a mistake we need to avoid before we get started on our plans for the new user experience."

EXAMPLE: PERSUASIVE PRESENTATION
Audience/outcome: A new business development executive seeks to win an advertising account from a prospective client, in the third link of a relationship she recently opened.

"According to Albert Einstein, 'Genius looks so much like hard work that it's tough to recognize.' As we have discussed, my team will deliver the 'big idea' to you. But it's time to acknowledge that genius isn't enough. We'll work late. Come in early. Double check the math. Dot the 'i's' and cross the 't's'. I'm Anna Gold, leader of the direct marketing team. Think of us as brains in overalls."

EXAMPLE: TEAM CONVERSATION
Audience/outcome: A project manager introduces himself in a team meeting when he wants to motivate everyone to do their part in relocating his company.

"Next to death and divorce, psychologists rank moving as the most stressful event in life. So, welcome to the first meeting of Stressed Anonymous. Hello, I'm Chris: stressed but ready to pack, lift, load and unload. I hope you are too!"

YOUR TURN

How do you plan to introduce yourself in your future interactions? Here are your choices:

- Heroic Achievement
- Startling Statistic
- Dramatic Quotation

ONWARD!

Onward to Great Opening, Segment Two!

Section Five

Act 1, Segment 2 (Introduce Your Topic)

WHAT'S IN THIS SECTION?

Chapter 14: Crime Story

Chapter 15: Epidemic Statistic

Chapter 16: Nugget

Chapter 17: Example or Analogy

Chapter 18: Success Story

ACT 1: GREAT OPENING
  Segment 1: Introduce Yourself
  Segment 2: Introduce Topic
  Segment 3: Make Promises
ACT 2: STREAMLINED CONTENT
  Segment 1: Foster Understanding
  Segment 2: Create Belief
  Segment 3: Ignite Urgency
ACT 3: GREAT CLOSING
  Segment 1: Recall Promises Kept
  Segment 2: Add Unexpected Value
  Segment 3: Give Instructions

Section Five
Key Concepts

AFTER YOU INTRODUCE YOURSELF, YOU INTRODUCE YOUR TOPIC AS A TEASE for your Streamlined Content in Act Two. Your ideal outcome is to compassionately connect to your audience's misery triggers. The ideal refrain in your audience's brain is: "Wow, this is so important, I want to hear more!"

Use one of these five alternatives to introduce your topic:

- **Crime Story:** Reveal how a problem was diagnosed and a solution discovered.
- **Epidemic Statistic:** Magnify looming consequences or illuminate the size of the problem.
- **Nugget:** Reveal a little known, one-of-a-kind, or time-sensitive fact about the problem.
- **Example or Analogy:** Provide a simple, easy to understand parallel to the problem your audience faces.
- **Success Story:** Provide a relatable case history with an enviable result.

Section Five
CHAPTER 14

Crime Story

Alternative #1 for a Great Opening, Segment Two (Introduce Your Topic)

T HE FIRST ALTERNATIVE FOR INTRODUCING YOUR TOPIC IS A CRIME Story. When your audience is already motivated to solve a problem, and you have relevant experience with a remedy for it, this is the perfect approach. It's a particularly effective way to establish why your audience should have confidence in your expertise, invention, discovery, or proprietary process, which you will reveal during Act Two.

CRIME STORIES MUST CONNECT TO YOUR AUDIENCE'S HEARTS AND MINDS

When your audience knows they have a problem, and you have an example featuring a "victim" they can relate to, this emotional approach to introducing your topic is perfect. That's how to engage their emotion and imagination. Their brains should be so busy visualizing and connecting to the colorful or heartfelt details; it is impossible for them to attend to any competing stimulation. Pick words that will wipe their minds clean of anything but your story.

FORMULA FOR A CRIME STORY

1. Your audience experiences the story—use "you."
2. Victims suffer misery—use action words.
3. A hero discovers the invention or delivers the system.
4. Tease your audience with your content's personal appeal and application.

EXAMPLE #1

"I don't know if you've ever seen a person injured in a chemical spill, but I can tell you that chemical burns are among the ugliest wounds a person can suffer. Until the government-imposed safety protocols, workers were often blinded, scalded, or disfigured because their workplaces had no emergency medical aid on the premises. When a family member was seriously injured in an acid spill on a metal processing production line, a Keck scientist took it upon himself to experiment with growing artificial skin cells. From that first personal mission, Keck has continued its dedication to developing leading-edge cures in dermatology. If you care about people—young and old—suffering from a skin disease, disorder, or condition, your life may be about to change."

Let's take that example step by step

Step 1: *Your audience experiences the story—use "you."*
"I don't know if you've ever seen a person injured in a chemical spill, but I can tell you that chemical burns are among the ugliest wounds a person can suffer."

Step 2: *Victims suffer misery—use action words*
"Until the government-imposed safety protocols, workers were often blinded, scalded, or disfigured because their workplaces had no emergency medical aid on the premises."

Step 3: *A hero discovers the invention or delivers the system*
"When a family member was seriously injured in an acid spill on a metal processing production line, a Keck scientist took it upon himself to experiment with growing artificial skin cells. From that first personal mission, Keck has continued its dedication to developing leading-edge cures in dermatology."

Step 4: *Tease your audience with your content's personal appeal and application*
"If you care about people—young and old—suffering from a skin disease, disorder, or condition, your life may be about to change."

EXAMPLE #2

"What if you had just one chance—the chance of your lifetime—to earn and put away all the money you would ever need to feel secure, to support yourself and your family, to live the life of your dreams? A farmer in Wichita Falls, Kansas, lost that chance when he went bankrupt because his crop failed and he could not pay the mortgage on his property. That man was my neighbor, someone who was good and decent and almost like a father to me. He became my inspiration for building a bank that was more than a debt collector. Does that sound like a bank you need?"

LET'S TAKE THAT EXAMPLE STEP BY STEP

Step 1: *Your audience experiences the story—use "you."*
"What if you had just one chance—the chance of your lifetime—to earn and put away all the money you would ever need to feel secure, to support yourself and your family, to live the life of your dreams?"

Step 2: *Victims suffer misery—use action words*
"A farmer in Wichita Falls, Kansas, lost that chance when he went bankrupt because his crop failed and he could not pay the mortgage on his property."

Step 3: *A hero discovers the invention or delivers the system*
"That man was my neighbor, someone who was good and decent and almost like a father to me. He became my inspiration for building a bank that was more than a debt collector."

Step 4: *Tease your audience with your content's personal appeal and application*
"He became my inspiration for building a bank that was more than a debt collector. Does that sound like a bank you need?"

ONWARD!
Let's progress to your second alternative for introducing your topic: epidemic statistics.

Section Five
CHAPTER 15

Epidemic Statistic

Alternative #2 for a Great Opening, Segment Two (Introduce Your Topic)

W HEN YOUR AUDIENCE UNDERESTIMATES A PROBLEM OR APPEARS to ignore it entirely, an Epidemic Statistic is perfect. In this alternative to introducing your topic, you raise concerns about the looming consequences of a problem and your approach to thwarting it or solving it. This approach is also helpful when your audience is embarrassed to admit they have a problem and you can show they are not alone.

NO SHAME, ALL GAIN

Choose an epidemic statistic when 1) your topic involves a problem your audience mistakenly perceives as a minor annoyance, or 2) they are afraid to admit they have the problem.

In business as in life, acknowledging a problem is the first step toward solving it. However, it's human nature to underestimate troubles or delay dealing with them until they balloon up so big they become a crisis. People tend to procrastinate, delay, and distract themselves instead of preventing or dealing with problems head-on.

So, if you or your solution depend on your audience grasping the brutal truth of their situation, an epidemic statistic is a great way to sensitively and respectfully amplify their pain, so they focus on it.

Unlike the positive statistic you use to introduce yourself in Segment One, now use a metric that makes it painfully clear a threatening situation looms. The goal is to help them see they can and should address their problem now. Include a reassuring coda that your upcoming content will provide a roadmap to a safe and satisfying solution. That will arouse their curiosity about how to diagnose or treat the problem they now feel ready to handle with your help.

Two types of situations call for an epidemic statistic as the ideal way to introduce your topic.

THE IGNORANCE IS BLISS GROUP

In this first case, your audience experiences a mildly irritating inconvenience, that has unforeseen negative consequences. They might be ignoring it, working around it, or simply accommodating it.

For example, accountants often work incredibly long hours during tax season. They never consider how the stress and lack of sleep profoundly impact their health.

They resist hiring temporary help or buying sophisticated tax planners for their clients to use, which would reduce their debilitating routine. Your job is to focus them on the statistical probability they will face negative health consequences from overworking before you deliver your content on how to change the way they manage their practice.

THE DON'T ASK, DON'T TELL CROWD

In this second scenario, you may have an audience who is fully aware of a problem and its magnitude, but they are embarrassed to admit what's wrong. Perhaps they made a mistake and feel it's unflattering to their image. Or, they believe if they publicly acknowledge a shortcoming, they might lose their jobs. For example, call center staff might be hanging up on difficult customers. Rather than ask for help in managing these callers, the staff hopes supervisors don't find out what they're doing wrong.

Your job is to give them the surprising news that they are making a common mistake. Rather than accuse them of being unfit or inappropriate, share a statistic to illustrate how many customer service representatives suffer from the same lack of skills.

At the end of your introduction to topic, let your audience know know it's easy to overcome this error if they follow your approach. Ideally, you can add how you helped other people successfully conquer the same or a similar problem. That ignites their interest in your upcoming content.

FORMULA FOR EPIDEMIC STATISTICS

1. Provide a metric or calculation of an overlooked or hidden problem.
2. Reveal its implications or how commonly it occurs.
3. Tease the remedy or relief coming up in your content.

EXAMPLE #1

The head of manufacturing addresses his team. He says:

"You may think our 98% defect-free rate of production is something to brag about. Right now, customers just pick out the defects and send them back. However, consider this. When we scale up to producing a million units, we'll be producing 20,000 defective components that infect our shipments. When that happens, customers will just refuse to take our units into inventory. What can we do to avert this catastrophe?"

LET'S TAKE THAT EXAMPLE STEP BY STEP

Step 1: *Provide a metric or calculation of the overlooked problem*
"You may think our 98% defect-free rate of production is something to brag about. Right now, customers just pick out the defects and send them back."

Step 2: *Reveal its implications*
"But consider this. When we scale up to producing a million units, we'll be producing 20,000 defective components that infect our shipments. When that happens, customers will just refuse to take our units into inventory."

Step 3: *Tease the remedy or relief coming up in your content*
"What can we do to avert this catastrophe?"

EXAMPLE #2

A software consultant speaks to business owners. She says:

"Do you think you are the only person left operating without the latest software or electronic devices? Do you think it's too difficult to learn how to use new technology or it's too expensive to upgrade? Three out of five small businesses are currently making the transition from old-style recordkeeping to today's technology. In my experience, every one of them has been successful within just two months of deciding to move ahead. What if I could guarantee your success and give you your money back if you did not get exactly the results you desire?"

Let's take that example step by step

Step 1: *Provide a metric or calculation of the overlooked problem*
"Do you think you are the only person left operating without the latest software or electronic devices? Do you think it's too difficult to learn how to use new technology or it would be too expensive to upgrade?"

Step 2: *Reveal how commonly the problem occurs*
"Three out of five small businesses are currently making the transition from old-style recordkeeping to today's technology. In my experience, every one of them has been successful within just two months of deciding to move ahead."

Step 3: *Tease the remedy or relief coming up in your content*
"What if I could guarantee your success and give you your money back if you did not get exactly the results you desire?"

ONWARD!
Let's progress to the third alternative for introducing your topic: nuggets.

Section Five
CHAPTER 16

Nugget

Alternative #3 for a Great Opening, Segment Two (Introduce Your Topic)

A NUGGET IS IDEAL WHEN YOU HAVE AN EXCLUSIVE, TIME-SENSITIVE tidbit that will intrigue your audience and get them to lean into your topic. It's a great way to refresh an audience's interest in an issue they previously dealt with, consider insolvable, or avoid because it is part of the status quo. Provide a fresh insight or a new pathway to avoid or remedy the issue.

DELIVER A JUICY TIDBIT

Choose the nugget when you're announcing something new: a product, process, employee, feature, opportunity, or service. Your nugget must reveal exclusive, one-of-a-kind, time-sensitive, newsworthy, or proprietary data. Whet the appetite of your audience. They'll want to know more about your content—specifically how they can apply your knowledge for their benefit or protection.

A NUGGET MAY BE THE MOST SATISFYING INTRODUCTION TO TOPIC

Most busy people believe they only have time for nuggets. Most people go to a meeting hoping for just one. Consider how often you have come away from even the most educational presentation and been able to keep only one or two nuggets in your head.

To introduce your topic, use a nugget whenever you have one. It should be your default introduction to topic because it is so universally appreciated.

FORMULA FOR A NUGGET

1. Report a credible source made an announcement.
2. Reveal the information.
3. Describe the benefits or implications of the news.
4. Tease your content's power to transform the audience.

EXAMPLE #1

"In December, the Kentucky Equine Education Project formally announced what many citizens of our state already know from their pay stubs: The Kentucky Derby is a $127 million payday for the state of Kentucky's economy. Racetracks and horse farms employ over 140,000 people. Even that number does not take into account other related companies and jobs— insurance, hospitality, media, and more—that serve the people in the horseracing industry. Every sector of business is represented. Why have so many companies come to the Bluegrass State? What do they know that you should know?"

LET'S TAKE THAT EXAMPLE STEP BY STEP

Step 1: *Report a credible source made an announcement*
"Kentucky Equine Education Project formally announced ..."

Step 2: *Reveal the information*
"racetracks and horse farms employ over 140,000 people."

Step 3: *Describe the benefits or implications of the news*
"That number does not take into account other related companies and jobs— insurance, hospitality, media, and more—that serve those people."

Step 4: *Tease your content's power to transform the audience*
"Why have all these companies flocked to the Bluegrass State? What do they know that you should know?"

EXAMPLE #2

"The National Association for the Education of Young Children revealed that one out of ten toddlers engages in biting behaviors. Most bites occur in September, and male toddlers initiate most episodes.

A child is more likely to get bitten if he or she is new to a group of students who are already enrolled in a class. Sending your child to school with familiar playmates and avoiding a late start in the semester are just two tips to safeguard your child's health and well-being. How many other vital facts about preschool do you need to know before you'll feel comfortable dropping your child off on the first day of school?"

Let's take that example step by step

Step 1: *Report a credible source made an announcement*
"The National Association for the Education of Young Children revealed ..."

Step 2: *Reveal the information*
"one out of ten toddlers engage in biting behaviors. Most bites occur in September, and male toddlers initiate most episodes. A child is more likely to get bitten if he or she is new to a group of students who are already enrolled in a class."

Step 3: *Describe the benefits or implications of the news*
"Sending your child to school with familiar playmates and avoiding a late start in the semester are just two tips to safeguard your child's health and well-being."

Step 4: *Tease your content's power to transform the audience*
"How many other vital facts about preschool do you need to know before you'll feel comfortable dropping your child off on the first day of school?"

ONWARD!
Let's progress to the fourth alternative for introducing your topic: examples and analogies.

Section Five
CHAPTER 17

Example or Analogy

Alternative #4 for a Great Opening, Segment Two (Introduce Your Topic)

WHEN YOUR TOPIC IS COMPLEX OR TECHNICAL EXPERTISE IS AT THE heart of diagnosing or fixing a problem, a surprising Example or Analogy is the best choice. Because it is perfect for an audience with unknown or varying levels of familiarity with terminology, this introduction will raise their curiosity and desire to engage with you. It's a perfect way to lower resistance.

YOU LOSE WHEN YOU CONFUSE THEM

When your audience is unfamiliar with your topic, or you're conducting a training session on technical material, you risk losing your audience's attention and trust. To help them grasp a complex concept, use an example or analogy to make your information accessible.

Most people feel anxious about learning, especially when it must be done while someone else is watching. The average learner fears everyone is smarter, more experienced, or just faster to grasp new information than they are. Your surprising example or analogy puts their mind at ease and allows them to pay attention by making a clear connection between something they already understand and the thing they are about to learn. When you add a surprising aspect, it delights as well as informs them.

FORMULA FOR EXAMPLE

1. Share the surprising example.
2. Make the connection to your topic.
3. Amplify your audience's anxiety or concern.
4. Tease the content you will deliver is transformative.

EXAMPLE: A SURPRISING EXAMPLE

"Is two scoops of gourmet ice cream a delicious dessert or a higher insurance premium? Calories are not simply what you put in your mouth—they are what determines your health, what's in your bank account, and often the quality of your family life—even your job opportunities. The magic you've been looking for when it comes to weight loss isn't in a pill or an exercise regimen. The magic comes from your mindset. If we can change the way you perceive food, you'll lose weight effortlessly and keep it off for the rest of your life."

Let's take that example step by step

Step 1: *Share the surprising example*
"Is two scoops of gourmet ice cream a delicious dessert or a higher insurance premium?"

Step 2: *Make the connection to your topic*
"Calories are not simply what you put in your mouth—they are what determines your health, what's in your bank account, and often the quality of your family life—even your job opportunities."

Step 3: *Amplify your audience's anxiety or concern*
"The magic you've been looking for when it comes to weight loss isn't in a pill or an exercise regimen."

Step 4: *Tease the content you will deliver is transformative*
"The magic comes from your mindset. If we can change the way you perceive food, you'll lose weight effortlessly and keep it off for the rest of your life."

FORMULA FOR A SURPRISING ANALOGY

1. Show two seemingly unrelated things are like one another.
2. Outline consequences or implications.
3. Amplify your audience's anxiety or concern.
4. Tease the content you will deliver is transformative.

EXAMPLE: SURPRISING ANALOGY

"Most people in business are like baby ducks: They learn how to act by watching someone else. The famous psychologist, Dr. Lorenz, proved that baby ducks imprint on the first thing they see, which is most often their mothers or fathers. That's why they walk like ducks. If they first saw a lion, well, they would walk like a lion—at least until the lion turned around and ate them. Early in your career, you may have imprinted on someone who had less than the best interpersonal skills. You may have unconsciously picked up bad habits in the way you deal with conflict, deadlines, and other stressors that naturally arise from working with other people. The good news is you can retrain your brain and learn to walk and talk—and act at work—precisely like the most successful people in the world if you have the right role-models in mind."

LET'S TAKE THAT EXAMPLE STEP BY STEP

Step 1: *Show two seemingly unrelated things are like one another*
"Most people in business are like baby ducks: They learn how to act by watching someone else. The famous psychologist, Dr. Lorenz, proved that baby ducks imprint on the first thing they see, which is most often their mothers or fathers."

Step 2: *Outline consequences or implications*
"That's why they walk like ducks. If they first saw a lion, well, they would walk like a lion ..."

Step 3: *Amplify audience's anxiety or concern*
"—at least until the lion turned around and ate them. Early in your career, you may have imprinted on someone who had less than the best interpersonal skills. You may have unconsciously picked up bad habits in the way you deal with conflict, deadlines, and other stressors that naturally arise from working with other people."

Step 4: *Tease that your content can transform your audience*
"The good news is you can retrain your brain and learn to walk and talk—and act at work—exactly like the most successful people in the world if you have the right role-models in mind."

ONWARD!
Let's progress to the fifth and final alternative for introducing your topic: success stories.

Section Five
CHAPTER 18

Success Story

Alternative #5 for a Great Opening, Segment Two (Introduce Your Topic)

A SUCCESS STORY IS THE BEST CHOICE WHEN YOUR AUDIENCE IS skeptical or unsure about how a new approach or a new person might suit them. This approach inspires their involvement because you feature a role-model who overcame a challenge with a solution your audience finds accessible. It's perfect for an audience that likes to follow trends or is risk-averse.

NOTHING BEATS SUCCESS

Choose a success story or brief case history when your audience has doubts about you or your topic. This approach is especially useful when an audience previously rejected your proposal, and you are making a second approach to win their approval for a project or purchase.

By sharing positive outcomes, you aren't arguing or criticizing. You are opening a window to a different point of view. Therefore, a success story is a great way to turn around a team that's going in the wrong direction. A brief case history is compelling when an audience is stuck and needs a new path to follow. If you can, feature a highly visible or revered person or organization that has enjoyed a great result with you or the approach you are going to recommend later in Act Two.

FORMULA FOR A SUCCESS STORY

1. Feature a well-known, respected or highly visible person or entity.
2. Share the details of their misery and how they overcame it.
3. Convey the lesson or unexpected cascade of benefits of the story.
4. Tease that your content will reveal a similar road to success.

EXAMPLE #1

"Mark Victor Hansen, the genius behind *Chicken Soup for the Soul* books, reportedly received more than 100 rejection letters from publishers who were certain no one wanted to read heartfelt stories about courage, tenacity, and other old-fashioned character traits. All the pessimism seems crazy now because over 500 million *Chicken Soup* books have been sold! So, kudos to the one brave publisher who went against the popular opinion that our society is too hip and moves too fast to sit down and enjoy an inspirational story.

Mark's path is proof that rejection may be the first sign of success. If what we offer significantly differs from what's current or trendy, many people might dissuade us from competing. However, getting almost universal resistance often means there is an opportunity no one else sees. We need courage to get beyond the opposition we're facing with our new product launch. Wouldn't you like to take advantage of the opportunity that's hidden from everyone else's view? Wouldn't you want to share in that success?"

LET'S TAKE THAT EXAMPLE STEP BY STEP

Step 1: *Feature a highly visible person or organization*
"Mark Victor Hansen, the genius behind the *Chicken Soup for the Soul* books ..."

Step 2: *Share the details of their misery and how they overcame it*
"reportedly received more than 100 rejection letters from publishers who were certain no one wanted to read heartfelt stories about courage, tenacity, and other old-fashioned character traits."

Step 3: *Convey the lesson or unexpected cascade of benefits of the story*
"All the pessimism seems crazy now because over 500 million *Chicken Soup* books have been sold! So, kudos to the one brave publisher who went against the popular opinion that our society is too hip and moves too fast to sit down and enjoy an inspirational story. Mark's path is proof that rejection may be the first sign of success. If what we offer significantly differs from what's current or trendy, many people might dissuade us from competing. However, getting almost universal resistance often means there is an opportunity no one else sees. We need courage to get beyond the opposition we're facing with our new product launch."

Step 4: *Tease that your content will reveal a similar road to success*
"Wouldn't you like to take advantage of the opportunity that's hidden from everyone else's view? Wouldn't you like to share in that success?"

EXAMPLE #2

"Tony Parinello is among the most famous and successful sales trainers in the world. He hosts a radio talk show on selling and provides online training through www.clubvito.com. Millions of people purchase his educational materials and listen to him for advice on selling. Like most sought-after experts, Tony started out getting some hard knocks in 'real life.' He began his sales career as a representative with Hewlett Packard (HP) in the 1970s. At that time, HP was little known and regularly up against IBM, then the giant in computer sales. Every sale Tony made totaled a quarter to a half-million dollars. That was big money then, and big money today. Tony earned all that income, while he had a terrible personal disadvantage. He was virtually deaf at the age of twenty-eight. He adapted by focusing intently on his prospects' faces, learning to read their lips and facial expressions. His prospects and customers enjoyed being the focus of his attention and were amazed at his powers of concentration. Tony's 'method' of selling proved to be better than his competition's, sale after sale after sale. One customer objected when Tony got hearing aids, because he no longer appeared to be so attentive!

You have your disadvantages—we all do. How would you like to discover what's surprisingly powerful and positive about you, and make that the foundation for your success with your prospects and customers?"

LET TAKE THAT EXAMPLE STEP BY STEP

Step 1: *Feature a well-known, respected, or highly visible person or entity*
"Tony Parinello is among the most famous and successful sales trainers in the world. He hosts a radio talk show on selling and provides online training through www.clubvito.com. Millions of people purchase his educational materials and listen to him for advice on selling. Like most sought-after experts, Tony started out getting some hard knocks in 'real life.' He began his sales career as a representative with Hewlett Packard (HP) in the 1970s. At that time, HP was little known and regularly up against IBM, then the giant in computer sales. Every sale Tony made totaled a quarter to a half-million dollars. That was big money then, and big money today."

Step 2: *Share the details of their misery and how they overcame it*
"Tony earned all that income, while he had a terrible personal disadvantage. He was virtually deaf at the age of twenty-eight. He adapted by focusing intently on his prospects' faces, learning to read their lips and facial expressions."

Step 3: *Convey the lesson or unexpected cascade of benefits of the story*
"His prospects and customers enjoyed being the focus of his attention and were amazed at his powers of concentration. Tony's "method" of selling proved to be better than his competition's, sale after sale after sale. One customer objected when Tony got hearing aids, because he no longer appeared to be so attentive!"

Step 4: *Tease that your content will reveal a similar road to success*
"You have your disadvantages—we all do. How would you like to discover what's surprisingly powerful and positive about you, and make that the foundation for your success with your prospects and customers?"

STACK UP YOUR STORIES

Develop a stack of stories that mirror the industries or conditions facing your audiences. Be ready to pull out the right one when you face resistance.

TIP FOR ANCHORING COMMITMENT FROM ACT ONE INTO ACT TWO

As you know, after delivering your Great Opening (Act One), you will launch into your Streamlined Content (Act Two). Here's a tip: Seed your Streamlined Content with some of the exact words, issues, and people you introduced during your Great Opening. As you deliver content, repeat language you used in your opening.

Players will instantly recall the excitement they felt about you and your topic. They'll remember why they were so motivated to listen. Watch for this technique on any broadcast of the television program 60 Minutes. At the beginning of the program, you get a tease for each of three segments—just a few seconds of the most compelling content they'll deliver during the actual program.

Later in the program, when each segment airs, you hear the exact quotes and see the same footage from the program's opening. They are tapping your brain, and saying, "Here it is: exactly what you were looking for!" Your attention is once again focused. You renew your commitment to stay tuned.

This tip works for any interaction. For example, my daughter, Molly Jo, served as the tour director for one of the premier horse farms in Kentucky. Each tour began in the stallion barn where six famous thoroughbreds stood in their impeccable, elegant stalls. Molly Jo included these words in her introduction to topic.

"We're going to learn a bit of history about the farm, then I'll introduce you to the six fine gentlemen around us, and finally, we'll go over to the breeding shed where we might see one of them at work."

When she launched her Streamlined Content, Molly revisited some of the language from her introduction to the topic. She would say: "Now let me introduce you to the first of these fine gentlemen."

ONWARD!

Congratulations! You have completed your review of all the alternatives for Segment Two of Act One. Now on to the Great Opening Segment Three!

Section Six

Act 1, Segment 3 (Make Promises)

WHAT'S IN THIS SECTION?

Chapter 19: Promises

ACT 1: GREAT OPENING
  Segment 1: Introduce Yourself
  Segment 2: Introduce Topic
  Segment 3: Make Promises
ACT 2: STREAMLINED CONTENT
  Segment 1: Foster Understanding
  Segment 2: Create Belief
  Segment 3: Ignite Urgency
ACT 3: GREAT CLOSING
  Segment 1: Recall Promises Kept
  Segment 2: Add Unexpected Value
  Segment 3: Give Instructions

Section Six
Key Concepts

IN THE LAST SEGMENT OF YOUR GREAT OPENING, YOU MAKE A PROMISE TO your audience about what they will be able to do by the end of your time together. Your ideal outcome is this refrain in your audience's brain: "Wow, this will empower me to solve a significant problem in my life!"

This section takes you through the significance of this segment, which secures your audience's attention for the rest of the presentation and establishes or deepens your relationship. Plus, your promises are a stealth way to get them ready to take action in your Great Closing.

You have a choice of three approaches to making promises.

"I promise you will …"

"I guarantee you will …"

"My commitment to you is …"

Section Six
CHAPTER 19

Promises

Great Opening, Segment Three (Make Promises)

T HIS CHAPTER DELVES INTO THE MOST PIVOTAL MOMENT OF YOUR presentation: promises. They function as your critical transition from Act One, your Great Opening to Act Two, your Streamlined Content. You ignite their commitment to listen attentively and engage with you for the balance of your time, as you lead the communication toward mutual gain.

THE POWER OF PROMISES

This is the pivot point of your presentation: making a promise about how you will use your time with the audience. Your promise has three important jobs.

1. It gives the audience hope you can alleviate their misery and, therefore, intensifies their engagement with your presentation.
2. It introduces the proximate outcome you set for your presentation, albeit in a stealth manner.
3. It deepens your relationship with the audience by creating an obligation on your part and activating their dependence on you.

Consider how crucial the timing is on your promise. It comes after you introduced yourself, focusing on your values, philosophy, or priorities. Then, you introduced your topic, compassionately concentrating on the audience's pain, fear, or craving. Thus, your audience is at a magical moment, the peak of great opportunity. They have begun to trust, like, and care about you—and believe you feel the same about them. This is the beginning of getting everything you want.

WHAT YOUR PROMISE SETS IN MOTION

Immediately after you make your promise, you start delivering your Streamlined Content in Act Two, when you share insights, skills, examples, or other tools they can use. Remember: relationships are made by making and keeping promises.

FORMULA FOR A PROMISE

1. Make a specific promise, commitment, or guarantee.
2. Tease how your content will empower your audience.
3. Add: "by the end of our time together today."

EXAMPLE OF A BUSINESS DEVELOPMENT PROMISE

At a trade show presentation, Olivia Anderson's proximate outcome is to set appointments only with qualified prospects in her audience. Her presentation is the way she ascertains who has the specific problems and budgets that fit the solutions she represents and sells.

Thus, her promise is: "I promise by the end of our time together today; you will be able to diagnose your system failure and set the right budget for a solution."

Olivia fulfills her promise in Act Two by administering her proprietary assessment, which is a list of questions that profile the type of failures common in the industry she serves. Plus, she gives relevant examples and case studies that show how her solutions resolved specific problems.

Her content is inspiring and motivating. Moreover, her audience's responses reveal whether they are qualified prospects. Thus, she knows who is worth pursuing. She can then create profitable relationship maps for her follow up interactions.

START WITH YOUR OUTCOME IN MIND

Before you craft your promise, consider what you want the audience to do at the end of your time together. Here is a range of proximate outcomes for various links on relationships maps, although yours may differ.

- Make the purchase
- Give you the purchase order
- Get you access to information that will help you make a proposal
- Reveal whether they are qualified
- Schedule the additional meetings you need to reach your goal
- Practice the training

- File reports correctly and on time
- Make calls as instructed
- Change behavior
- Authorize the project

PLAN THEIR JOURNEY FROM RESISTANCE TO ACTION

In effect, your presentation is a journey from where they are before you start to where you want them to be at the end of your time together, taking action as you desire. Your promise is the lynchpin.

Emphasize they are going to DO something by virtue of your presentation—not just learn or get information. Why? You will get the greatest attention and compliance if players believe they will be empowered rather than educated.

HERE'S HOW TO START IDEATING ABOUT YOUR PROMISE

1. Consider their misery triggers.
2. Select the action you want them to take at this link on your relationship map. That is your proximate outcome.
3. Identify what they would need to discover and do before that action would seem attractive to them.
4. Consider what future actions or interactions you need to set up while you are with them in this link.

ASK YOURSELF THESE QUESTIONS

1. What is their current mindset and the ideal meeting style to transform their resistance, indifference, or inactivity?
   Negative to positive = Persuasive style
   Ignorant to competent = Training style
   Selfish to group-goal oriented = Team style
   Stuck to proactive = Briefing style
2. What do they lack that will help make it clear they should move forward with you? Consider what you can provide regarding insights, case histories, assessments, tips, facts, skills, and more.

Check out the Library of Success to help you brainstorm, select, or craft content. It shows which content works best for each meeting style and over 50 different components you can use for content.

READY, SET, PLAN TO PROMISE

A workplan that addresses these elements will be helpful in crafting promises that create and build relationships. Typically, your workplan will identify:

1. Your role
2. Audience profile
3. Your outcomes: relationship, gateway, and proximate
4. Desired actions in your Great Closing
5. Commitment to future actions in your Great Closing
6. Audience transformation: current resistant mindset to compliant mindset
7. Content components to assure transformation occurs
8. Promise that sets up mutual gain

SAMPLE WORKPLANS FOR MAKING AND FULFILLING PROMISES

As you review these examples, you'll see how promises are created based on the outcomes you desire. You'll also see how to quickly outline content components for Act Two, using codes from the Library of Success, so you are confident you can:

1. Fulfill your promises
2. Transform an audience from resistant to compliant
3. Get action and future commitments

EXAMPLE #1: PERSUASIVE-STYLE PRESENTATION WORKPLAN

Technical sales representative Lynn Finerman meets with a prospect.

Proximate Outcome and Gateway Outcome

Lynn sells testing and measurement equipment and upgrades to a plant manager in the third linked interaction of a prospect relationship map. Her outcome is to secure her first order from him.

Relationship Outcomes

Company: Build a key account to increase revenue and visibility in the market.
Personal: Meet quota and avoid losing territory.

ACTIONS PLANNED FOR GREAT CLOSING

1. Plant manager reviews and approves her assessment of the facility.
2. He selects off-the-shelf equipment shown in her online catalog.
3. He signs the agreement for purchase and installation.
4. He phones the purchasing department to cut the purchase order.

COMMITMENT PLANNED FOR GREAT CLOSING

Plant manager makes a note to meet with her boss about custom upgrades.

AUDIENCE MINDSET TRANSFORMATION

Current resistant mindset: Moderately negative about the purchase because a) he's not entirely convinced it will perform as promised, and b) he thinks it may be difficult to install.

DESIRED COMPLIANT MINDSET

Enthusiastically endorses purchase because he's convinced: a) the data proves the product delivers results, and b) installation can be accomplished during a scheduled shutdown.

TO IGNITE TRANSFORMATION

1. Prove that without the consistent, accurate testing and measurement only her product provides, a system easily falls out of specification, resulting in disaster (including when the competition's products are in place).
2. Demonstrate that her product remedies the pain and fulfills the desires of plant managers with similar time constraints for installation and even more complex configurations of the product.

CONTENT COMPONENTS FOR ACT TWO: STREAMLINED CONTENT

1. Motivating misery triggers (MM): Play video of damage plants suffered when systems fell out of specification
2. Props (PS): Show core cuts of damaged parts
3. Third-party standards (TH): Share the latest independent industry standards for measurement

4. Comparison to competition (CC): Use graphic illustrating the system measurements produced by her equipment compared to competition's less precise results
5. Success stories (SS): Illustrate ease of installation and use in other plants
6. Question guide (QS): Pose questions to evaluate plant readiness

Great Opening Segment Three: Make Promises

"By using the industry's new diagnostic form to assess your own system, I guarantee you'll leave this meeting completely confident you can fix your problem with the right-sized solution."

What NOT to Say

"You must understand that your steam will continue to go downhill in quality because your current setup isn't really working. You need to purchase our company's equipment if you want to avoid disaster."

EXAMPLE #2: TRAINING-STYLE PRESENTATION

IT database manager Gary Singleton meets with sales representatives.

Relationship Outcomes

Company: Sales representatives will:
1. Meet or exceed quota.
2. Use their time more effectively.
3. Be self-sufficient whenever possible because headquarters staff is not easily accessible in every time zone during business hours.

Personal: Gary will become a full-time trainer in the HR department

Proximate Outcome

Gary wants sales reps to learn how to use a new database to generate high-quality leads and stop bothering administrative support staff to do it for them.

Actions Planned for Great Closing

1. Each rep locates five prospects during the fifteen-minute, hands-on practice time with the database.
2. Reps in the learning lab print out the lead list and hand it to the trainer.
3. Reps attending from remote locations email their lead lists to him before signing off the e-meeting.

Commitments Planned for Great Closing
1. Reps access the system to generate quality leads every week.
2. Reps will report problems to Gary if they cannot use the system.

Audience Transformation
Current Resistant Mindset: Ignorant about the database. Most veterans resist using it because they are deficient in search skills.

Desired Compliant Mindset
Proficient in search skills and motivated by the power the database gives them to generate leads and revenue.

To Ignite Transformation
1. Prove the database is easy to use.
2. Be compatible with their self-interest, emphasizing the values of empowerment and security.

Content Components for Act Two:
Streamlined Content
1. Success story (SS): Testimony from a rep who uses the database and has seen his revenue skyrocket in an accelerated period of time
2. Animation (GA): Show how to create the database
3. Demonstration (PD): Model how to access the database to produce leads
4. Step-by-step instructions (ST): Share bullet-pointed guide to using the database
5. Hands-on practice (HO): Give each rep a tutorial based on their territory
6. Assessment (AS): Show how to generate lead forms

Great Opening Segment Three: Make Promises
"Today you'll tap into the database and discover a fast and easy way to increase and accelerate your revenue production. I promise that by the time we conclude today, you'll have a list of customers in your territory who are ready to purchase upgrades and who will welcome your call. I also guarantee you'll locate at least three strong prospects with a link to your current accounts—they're in sister companies. You'll become a master at generating the most profitable leads and be able to meet and exceed your quota."

WHAT NOT TO SAY

"Today you will learn how the database is organized and receive instruction in the search protocol. We're putting you through this training, so you can do more for yourself and stop relying on administrative staff because their time is better spent doing other things."

EXAMPLE #3: TEAM-STYLE MEETING WORKPLAN

Account supervisor Jack Hansen meets with employees and contractors.

RELATIONSHIP OUTCOMES

Company: Satisfy a profitable client of the agency.
Personal: Earn promotion to vice-president, account management.

PROXIMATE OUTCOME

Jack wants his staff to deliver the finished storyboard for the client's infomercial and keep the production schedule on time, the content on target with the objectives, and the project on budget.

RESULTS PLANNED FOR GREAT CLOSING

1. Each player lists the obstacles and specific solutions with deadlines for implementation.
2. Each player indicates his or her work product on a roadmap that has milestones along a timeline. Note: The map is on a whiteboard that produces paper copies each player receives before leaving.

ACTIONS PLANNED FOR GREAT CLOSING

1. Each player signs the contract of completion, showing the revised roadmap.
2. Once all the players have signed it, they each receive a copy of it.

AUDIENCE MINDSET TRANSFORMATION, AUDIENCE 1

Creative Staff: Copywriter, Art Director and Production Designer
Current resistant mindset: Distracted by projects for other agency clients.

DESIRED COMPLIANT MINDSET

Mission-focused, motivated by the: a) attention they receive, b) challenge of this project, and c) respect shown for their creative needs and output.

TO IGNITE TRANSFORMATION

Content must connect feelings of self-esteem and social approval to cooperation and compliance.

AUDIENCE MINDSET TRANSFORMATION, AUDIENCE 2

Business and Production Staff: Product Manager, Producer, and Director
Current Resistant Mindset: Disconnected because they are freelance and have other clients and income.

DESIRED COMPLIANT MINDSET

United with each other and the creative staff because their cooperation ensures: a) accelerated compensation as a result of the compressed schedule, and b) a showcase-quality work sample.

TO IGNITE TRANSFORMATION

Content must prove the roadmaps and timelines are achievable, and the payoff is guaranteed.

CONTENT COMPONENTS FOR ACT TWO:
STREAMLINED CONTENT

1. Sketch of roadmaps and timelines (RT): Show proposed schedule
2. Samples (SA): Share agency's past work produced in a similar fashion
3. Question guide (QS): Questions to identify obstacles and solutions
4. Resources (RS): Identify off-the-shelf software, art, media sources
5. Contract (CN): Show terms with the bonus for on-time completion

GREAT OPENING SEGMENT THREE: MAKE PROMISES

"I promise this meeting will pay off by giving you exactly what you desire from this project. We will reframe the work plan, so it accurately reflects the time and support you need. You'll have the opportunity to talk about the obstacles facing you, and we'll identify the resources or exchange information to overcome those obstacles. Before we leave, you'll approve a roadmap that guarantees you get what you need with minimum stress and maximum speed."

What NOT to Say

"This project has fallen apart because we're not talking to each other and no one seems to care that we might lose this client. It's time to remember why you were hired on this project and get your work done."

EXAMPLE #4: BRIEFING-STYLE MEETING WORKPLAN

Call center supervisor Ken MacDonald meets with his CEO and CFO.

Relationship Outcomes

Company: A 33% improvement in call center productivity
Personal: Job security

Proximate Outcome

Call center supervisor Ken MacDonald is seeking clear-cut authority from his CEO and CFO to implement his proposed changes without further collaboration with other employees or additional review from consultants.

Actions Planned for Great Closing

The CEO signs the work order, giving Ken authority to reorganize operator shifts and implement the proposed changes in policies and procedures that do not require additional funds.

CEO phones the ad agency account executive, directing them to make changes to the website and promotional materials as Ken desires.

Commitments Planned for Great Closing

1. CEO and CFO calendar a review of the changes that require funding.
2. They email responses to Ken within the week.

Mindset Transformation, Audience 1

CEO

Current Resistant Mindset: Partially informed about whether current policies, procedures, and materials are adequate for reaching company goals.

Desired Compliant Mindset

Fully updated and convinced a) the call center requires immediate, corrective action, and b) Ken's proposed remedy is simple to implement and will be effective.

CONTENT GOALS TO IGNITE TRANSFORMATION

Illustrate the looming consequence of not dealing with the pain, which is a continuing, precipitous decline in call center productivity.

MINDSET TRANSFORMATION, AUDIENCE 2

CFO

Current Resistant Mindset: Unsure whether paying for professional creative services will get a much better website than asking in-house personnel to do the work.

DESIRED COMPLIANT MINDSET

Motivated to hire the ad agency because he sees its websites are proven to produce desirable ROIs.

CONTENT GOALS TO IGNITE TRANSFORMATION

Prove the ROI will be rapid as a result of the new telesales script and the website ordering page will exceed the center's daily inbound volume goals within one week of implementation.

CONTENT COMPONENTS FOR ACT TWO:

STREAMLINED CONTENT

1. Motivating misery triggers (MM): Show line chart of call center's last six months of poor performance and the projected decline
2. Success stories (SS): Feature other centers' policies and procedures with their exemplary results stated in measurable terms
3. Samples (SA): Show ad agency's past creative work associated with ROI statistics
4. Graphic (GA): Represent the proposed system configurations as a simple modification
5. Roadmap and timeline (RT): Share initial proposal for implementation

GREAT OPENING SEGMENT THREE: MAKE PROMISES

"By the conclusion of this briefing, you may make a 33% improvement in our call center's productivity by authorizing a limited set of actions. I promise you'll be pleased to discover that most measures require no funding. Plus, the new program delivers a very attractive and proven ROI."

WHAT NOT TO SAY

"Today, you will understand the call center needs to be reorganized. We must change how we supervise operators because these people are either lazy or stupid—they just can't get it right. The current phone script and web ordering page are terrible."

CONGRATULATIONS! YOU MADE IT PAST THE FIRST MILESTONE!

Now you're ready to dig deeper into the strategy and tactics of the SPEAK UP SYSTEM Act Two: Streamlined Content.

Section Seven

Act 2, Segment 1 (Foster Understanding)

WHAT'S IN THIS SECTION?

Chapter 20: Logic, Demos, Insights

ACT 1: GREAT OPENING

Segment 1: Introduce Yourself

Segment 2: Introduce Topic

Segment 3: Make Promises

ACT 2: STREAMLINED CONTENT

Segment 1: Foster Understanding

Segment 2: Create Belief

Segment 3: Ignite Urgency

ACT 3: GREAT CLOSING

Segment 1: Recall Promises Kept

Segment 2: Add Unexpected Value

Segment 3: Give Instructions

Section Seven
Key Concepts

ACT TWO OF THE SPEAK UP SYSTEM LAUNCHES THE "KNOW-LIKE-IGNITE" stages of the Transformation Channel. Your goal is to deliver on your promises, deepen the relationship, and get your audience eager to take action.

This section explores the alternative ways to foster understanding, which is the purpose of Segment One of your Streamlined Content in the SPEAK UP SYSTEM. As a communication leader, you respectfully acknowledge your audience may not have all the necessary foundational principles and details they should consider.

How do you foster understanding? Provide credible, transparent, objective, and easy to follow background information. Frequently with this approach, you awaken the audience's agreement with your perspective without raising their resistance. Your ideal lead-off component should be significant, fresh, and sensitive to the audience's feelings. Then, add additional content components, depending on the amount of time you have with your audience.

Your ideal outcome is this refrain in your audience's brain: "Wow, now I fully understand the situation!"

To foster understanding, you may find the best content in these sections from the Library of Success: Logic, Demonstrations, and Insights. For more details and examples of content components, see the Library of Success at NanceSpeaks.com.

Section Seven
CHAPTER 20

Logic, Demos, Insights
Components for Streamlined Content, Segment One (Understanding)

T O FOSTER UNDERSTANDING, PROVIDE YOUR AUDIENCE WITH NEW information. Avoid selling, which will raise resistance. Impress them with clear, helpful, and provable facts. Educate them using trustworthy sources. Involve them in discovery activities. Present the material in attractive and accessible ways. Let them see you have prepared the appropriate background data, so they feel ready and eager to start evaluating how to solve their problem. Three ways to foster understanding follow.

LOGIC

Logic is fact-based, sound reasoning that is easy to follow and makes sense. Use content associated with logic when you need to show clear, objective, credible, and well-documented information that sets a solid foundation for your solution or approach.

Content components associated with logic you might have in your Library of Success include:

1. Blueprints
2. Data with Objective Analysis
3. Facts and Figures
4. Technical Data
5. Technical Drawings

DESCRIPTIONS

BLUEPRINTS

A blueprint shows the audience how to build a design for a building, physical structure, or even a product. The term "blueprint" is also used to talk more generally about a systematic approach that can be used to replicate a proven process or method.

DATA WITH OBJECTIVE ANALYSIS

Primary research with metrics or a collection of responses from a focus group and secondary research from previously conducted studies can quickly bring an audience up to date. You may provide unbiased commentary, directing their attention to striking, new findings.

FACTS AND FIGURES

You may display information you have collected, observed, or verified by using charts, graphs, and lists. The goal is to help your audience grasp essential information they may be missing or overlooking in terms of its magnitude or importance.

TECHNICAL DATA

Precise dimensions, calculations based on equations, measurements, flow rates, or other findings based on expert knowledge may be useful in setting the stage for comparisons or recommendations you make later on in your presentation.

TECHNICAL DRAWINGS

When you want to show how a design works or focus the audience on a specific part of a process, a detailed illustration with "call-outs" provides the necessary details to help an audience understand specific, granular features, or facets.

DEMONSTRATIONS

Use demonstrations whenever it's possible for your audience to watch a product in action or see a process, test, proceeding, or approach. Their eye-witness alleviates the pressure for them to have faith in your impressions or opinion. They can "see it to believe it."

Content Components for demonstrations might include:

1. Features, Functions, and Performance
2. Product Demonstrations
3. Proprietary Processes or Parts
4. Samples

DESCRIPTIONS

FEATURES, FUNCTIONS, AND PERFORMANCE

Showcase the various parts, attributes, core cuts, operating elements, and critical aspects of your product, service, or method. You can explain how something works by focusing on specific components of a system or machine.

PRODUCT DEMONSTRATIONS

Focus on the performance or operation of a product or method, from a user's point of view. Your demonstration may be done live, on video, or through virtual reality. Customers are more likely to purchase a product or service they see in action because they witness the potential benefits and can be "talked through" its limitations.

PROPRIETARY PROCESSES OR PARTS

Highlight what your audience could not get from another source. A company or inventor typically has ownership or exclusive rights to any product or process that they develop. Due to the research and technology involved, trademark, copyright, or patents may apply. You might also have "know-how" or expertise that is not genuinely intellectual property but differentiates you or your organization in an impressive way.

SAMPLES

An audience can often infer the quality and function of an actual product if you supply a small, representative quantity of a product or service. Usually offered for free or at a vastly discounted rate, samples are a way to acquaint a prospective customer with your product, service, or brand. Whenever you can, provide a small bite, taste, color chip, or other means for an audience to get involved with your product or service.

INSIGHTS

Help your audience integrate the meaning of information, by seeing an angle or perspective that might not be obvious to them. To provoke insights, you might use credible and trustworthy sources who have an expert opinion. Alternatively, you may get creative and use insights to spark your audience's imagination. Stay credible and trustworthy as you use these components.

Content Components for insights you might have in your Library of Success include:

1. Analogies
2. Examples
3. Graphics, Photos, Animation, and Artwork
4. Props
5. Recommendations and References
6. Resources
7. Video and Audio

DESCRIPTIONS

Analogies

An analogy is a comparison between two different things that have similar qualities. Analogies help your audience relate to your content even if they are unfamiliar with the topic or the material is challenging. For example, water flowing through a hose is a good analogy for air flowing in the human body through the trachea and bronchi. It's likely your audience knows that a kink in a hose stops the flow of water. Hence a block in the windpipe stops airflow. In the business sphere, analogies help with idea generation and problem-solving.

Examples

When you have a long or complicated concept to explain, an example can instantly clarify your point. Examples also enliven a mundane subject. Explore or highlight a specific case so your audience can relate to a theory or idea or see how it's put to use.

Graphics, Photo, Animation, and Artwork

Colorful images, black and white line drawings, cartoons, pictures, and other creative, highly visual ways to display information are useful in keeping your audience engaged. Visuals often crystallize a concept or help illustrate what you want your audience to know.

Props

An item used to represent something else or an empty or non-working version of a product would be a prop. Use a prop when the actual item would be too big, heavy, delicate, or dangerous to use out of its element or installation. It's meant to help your audience visualize your narrative.

Recommendations and References
Letters of support, endorsements, or citations from reputable sources often provide instant credibility. These are valuable when a customer is unsure of a product's capability or your experience. Often references are not presented but simply highlighted when you are speaking and then handed-out for the audience's later review.

Resources
An audience often feels more comfortable with limited information when they know they can access additional support when they need it. When you have it, highlight your help desk access, support centers, or on-demand material and content. Access to expert personnel may be among the resources you can offer to an audience.

Video and Audio
Multimedia is useful when motion or sound is necessary for an audience to understand your subject. For example, if you are discussing particular geography or terrain, noise, or something you cannot recreate in front of an audience, a video or audio clip will get your information across. This is useful for product demonstrations and other times when you want your audience to see something in action.

ONWARD
Now let's move on to the second segment of your Streamlined Content: create belief.

Section Eight

Act 2, Segment 2 (Create Belief)

Chapter 21: Create Belief

ACT 1: GREAT OPENING
  Segment 1: Introduce Yourself
  Segment 2: Introduce Topic
  Segment 3: Make Promises
ACT 2: STREAMLINED CONTENT
  Segment 1: Foster Understanding
  Segment 2: Create Belief
  Segment 3: Ignite Urgency
ACT 3: GREAT CLOSING
  Segment 1: Recall Promises Kept
  Segment 2: Add Unexpected Value
  Segment 3: Give Instructions

Section Eight
Key Concepts

IN THIS SECOND SEGMENT OF YOUR STREAMLINED CONTENT, YOU CREATE THE belief your solution or approach is superior, right-sized, and coming at the perfect time. Your ideal outcome is this refrain in your audience's brain: "Wow, I believe your solution is the best!"

You are still guiding the audience through the "know-like-ignite" stages of the Transformation Channel. You just delivered knowledge to foster a new understanding of the situation.

To create belief, you may find the best content in these sections of the Library of Success: Comparisons, Credibility, Downsides, and Inspiration.

Section Eight

CHAPTER 21

Comparisons, Downsides, Credibility, Inspiration

Components for Streamlined Content, Segment Two (Belief)

To create belief, help your audience discover different ways to solve their problem.

Avoid strident advocacy, which often raises resistance. An excellent way to underscore your trustworthy nature is presenting a set of three choices, leveraging the "Goldilocks Principle." Rather than disrespect or denigrate competing options, describe them as good for other audiences. Then, share content showing why your recommendation is best suited to your audience.

Four ways to create belief follow.

COMPARISONS

Comparing alternatives based on meaningful differences helps your audience evaluate different features, functions, benefits, consequences, symbolism, and other characteristics of a range of solutions. Be respectful when you speak about competition or alternatives. When you are an advocate for one approach, such as what you are selling, address why your competition is better for companies or individuals with different challenges, conditions, or goals than your audience has.

Content components associated with comparisons you might have in your Library of Success include:

1. Comparison of Alternatives
2. Comparison of Competition

DESCRIPTIONS

COMPARISON OF ALTERNATIVES

Presenting an array of different courses of action helps your audience trust your leadership. Before committing, a decision-maker typically will seek out, examine, and compare the available options. To show you are aligned, help determine criteria that matter in getting the results your audience seeks, including facets they may not have previously identified. For example, consider the long-term impact of economic, social, political, and environmental factors on your audience. Perhaps you can point to an exclusive, valuable cascade of benefits that flow from your solution. As you select options to present, remember your audience may be considering little or no change to the status quo.

COMPARISON OF COMPETITION

Once a course of action is determined, you may initiate an examination of how to enact it using one solution versus others. With the audience's goals in mind, contrast what solutions are available and how they fit the most important criteria for success. Often a graphic depiction of choices is helpful. For example, create a chart that lists relevant standards and shows how each competitor measures up. You may list features, functions, performance, and benefits of your diverse product line, or how you compare to your direct and indirect competition and product substitutes.

DOWNSIDES

Downsides illuminate potential negative aspects or fallout that might occur from a decision. Ill effects are often part of a necessary, responsible, and respectful discussion. Bring them up, so you appear to be fair, honest, intelligent, and reliable.

Content components associated with downsides you might have in your Library of Success include:

1. Contrary Data or Conclusions
2. Plan Bs
3. Risk Analysis

DESCRIPTIONS

CONTRARY DATA OR CONCLUSIONS

Information that conflicts with the data you presented, differing assumptions, or alternative conclusions may be appropriate to share when you help an audience see the potential downside of a decision and course of action. Often circumstances are dynamic, and decision makers lack full visibility into the total universe of facts. A trustworthy and compassionate speaker seeks to give as complete a picture as possible, along with alternate ways to address conflicting information. Based on independent or historical sources, you may share the probability other data is correct or predict the likelihood that an assessment different than your own could occur.

PLAN BS

Plan B refers to secondary or alternative options that go into effect when the first course of action fails or doesn't go as planned. These contingencies should provide peace of mind and limit anxiety, by allowing management to have clear courses of action at the ready in moments of uncertainty and times of crisis. Proactive problem-solving underscores how trustworthy you are. For example, a facilities manager may advocate for building the safest elevators but in the case of an earthquake, typically wants residents to have a clear path to stairways.

RISK ANALYSIS

Risk analysis is the process by which a company investigates, identifies, and analyzes the issues that could negatively affect the outcome of a project or objective. It also allows the organization to develop strategies and assess the benefits versus the potential liabilities of a course of action. This evaluation often helps a company avoid or reduce the impact of potentially harmful factors. When it's appropriate, provide the proper calculations, references, case histories, and other material to help decision-makers evaluate their current and future situation.

CREDIBILITY

Credibility comes from independent sources that corroborate, endorse, support, or otherwise vouch for you or your approach and solution. Cite respected, relevant people and organizations. When you are seeking to create belief in the choice you prefer, provide role-models and other reference points as proof your audience is in good company.

Content components associated with credibility you might have in your Library of Success include:

1. People Profiles
2. References
3. Testimonials and Endorsements
4. Third Party Standards and Evaluations

DESCRIPTIONS

People Profiles

A profile is a summary of available data collected about a person, such as a biography. This historical record of education, experience, and achievement can get very detailed, even taking into account attitudes, habits, hobbies, and beliefs. These biographical sketches are often used to establish credibility or familiarize your audience with key individuals. A professional photo often called a "headshot," raises your audience's sense of connection and confidence.

References

Reference material may include a published journal article, a speech from a noted expert, or an esteemed person's opinion. Use this to help clarify a point you are making or provide additional support for a theory, position, or your qualifications. A resume or document listing achievements could be valuable reference material. A company may also develop a reference guide to illustrate the benefits, features, and uses for a product or product line.

Testimonials and Endorsements

Personal experience communicated through recommendations for a product, service, claim, or individual is often useful in creating belief. You might include promotional statements, such as critical acclaim for a new technology or a seal of approval from a respected organization. A celebrity endorsement of a product or testimony about its effectiveness can instantly enhance attractiveness.

THIRD PARTY STANDARDS AND EVALUATIONS

An independent review of your product or service, based on criteria generally accepted or respected by your audience is almost always desirable. Certifications from an institution, unbiased board, industry group, or regulator; or meeting impartial standards and requirements for goods, services, or business practices are big credibility boosters. When you present an innovation, it is often helpful to show an esteemed association, analyst, or independent board's future roadmap to illustrate how your invention aligns with respected forecasts.

INSPIRATION

Inspirational content sparks a positive emotional response to your information. Produce or arouse a hopeful, optimistic point of view by citing rewards of employing your solution. If it's inspiring, share your motivation and details about how you arrived at your position or recommendation.

Content components associated with inspiration you might have in your Library of Success include:

1. Applications and Use Cases
2. Case Histories
3. Invention or Discovery Stories
4. Motivating Misery Trigger Stories
5. Rewards and Results Lists
6. Success Stories

APPLICATIONS AND USE CASES

An application or use case typically showcases a specific installation of a product or service that can be employed in several industries or different conditions. For example, nuclear power plants, natural gas refineries, and oil drilling all use industrial valves. An application would be a review of the valve in just one of those areas, that being the one most closely related to your audience.

CASE HISTORIES

A case history is a clinical approach to storytelling. It lays out the biography or situation analysis before engaging with a solution and then details some aspects of the intervention. Finally, it may provide an update on the post-treatment regimen. While it may not involve medicine or healthcare, it is easy to see why a case history is an excellent teaching or reporting tool in that profession.

Invention or Discovery Stories

Sharing the story behind an innovation or breakthrough can be more cap-
tivating than merely showcasing the invention. An individual's unusual or
unexpected background allows the audience to make a personal connection
to a product, service or individual, inspiring a deeper relationship. You might
highlight why your company founders opened the firm, why your products or
services were developed, and what hardships were overcome to create them.
For example, the technology behind an ATM is impressive; however, the reason
it was invented—to give bank employees a fair work week and anxious bank
customers access to their funds anytime—is more compelling.

Motivating Misery Trigger Stories

If it's appropriate to remind the audience of their pain, fear, and craving, you
may introduce a story that highlights how distressing a problem is to their
organization or one just like it. It can be especially eye-opening to focus on the
downstream consequences of what seems like a slight inconvenience, minor
difficulty, or niggling wish. Almost every small misery presents an excellent
opportunity for you to present the benefits of your skills, products, plans, or
point-of-view. For example, managers often ignore intermittent failure, yet in
a mission-critical area such as IT, you might warn them an outage can cause
havoc. Thus, you spark the belief it's time to solve the issue.

Rewards and Results Lists

Outlining the benefits and positive outcomes of taking action is often more
powerful than merely explaining features and functions. You may surprise
your audience with unexpected benefits to heighten their desire to remedy a
problem with your solution. For example, a healthy diet improves mood and
energy, combats disease, and might even affect employment opportunity, all
while it also reduces weight and size.

Success Stories

A success story is social proof that you, or your product or services, perform
well under the conditions related to your audience's situation. By describing
a specific case with details about its requirements, hurdles, and methods, you
can use real-life experience to reassure your audience they are making the
right choice by taking your recommendation. Typically, "before" and "after"
pictures boost their belief that your option is both effective and attractive.

ONWARD!

Now let's move forward to the third and last segment of your Streamlined Content: ignite urgency and the fear of missing out.

Section Nine

Act 2, Segment 3 (Ignite Urgency)

WHAT'S IN THIS SECTION?

Chapter 22: Interactivity, Tips, Accountability

ACT 1: GREAT OPENING
Segment 1: Introduce Yourself
Segment 2: Introduce Topic
Segment 3: Make Promises
ACT 2: STREAMLINED CONTENT
Segment 1: Foster Understanding
Segment 2: Create Belief
Segment 3: Ignite Urgency
ACT 3: GREAT CLOSING
Segment 1: Recall Promises Kept
Segment 2: Add Unexpected Value
Segment 3: Give Instructions

Section Nine
Key Concepts

IN THIS THIRD AND LAST SEGMENT OF YOUR STREAMLINED CONTENT, YOU ignite your audience's desire to act now. The ideal outcome is this refrain in their brain: "Wow! I don't want to make a mistake and miss out on this opportunity!"

To ignite urgency, you may find the best content in these sections of the Library of Success: Interactivity, Tips, and Accountability.

Section Nine

CHAPTER 22

ACT 2: STREAMLINED CONTENT
Segment 1: Foster Understanding
Segment 2: Create Belief
Segment 3: Ignite Urgency

Interactivity, Tips, Accountability

Components for Streamlined Content, Segment Three (Ignite Urgency)

W HEN YOU IGNITE URGENCY, YOU ARE GUIDING YOUR AUDIENCE through the last stage of the "know-like-ignite" sequence of the Transformation Channel.

By the end of this segment, they must fear missing out. For example, if your audience took an assessment, have them self-grade it and review the results. The grading key would point out looming consequences if they fail to take immediate action. You might also go over budgets and other financial documentation that show how your solution fits into their plans.

Also (if you can), offer a valuable, limited time incentive. Tease it as a one-time opportunity, only provided in THIS interaction. Consider offering one of these incentives: a bundle of products offered at a special price, access to premium features or limited inventory, extra technical support, or acceptance into a beta or pilot program. You might offer preferred scheduling or no-cost delivery. Unless they ask, wait until your Great Closing to give instructions about how to take advantage of your offer.

Three ways of igniting urgency follow.

INTERACTIVITY

Interactivity personally engages your audience. Involve them in a dialogue. Encourage them to examine or ponder the details involved in decision making while they are with you. If it makes sense, give them the opportunity to touch, taste, feel, smell, see, or otherwise experience your solution or its benefits. Spark their conviction your solution is ideal.

Content components associated with interactivity you might have in your Library of Success include:

1. Assessments
2. Audience Experiences
3. Hands-on Practice
4. Questions and Answers
5. Role-play

DESCRIPTIONS

ASSESSMENTS

Personalize your content with a quiz or appraisal that helps each member of your audience evaluate their performance, expertise, or processes, as it relates to your solution. This component is particularly useful in fulfilling the promise you made in your Great Opening. They can put your content to use and self-diagnose the gap between their real situation and their ideal one. Provide a self-grading key, so their responses immediately underscore what they are lacking or missing.

AUDIENCE EXPERIENCES

Immerse your audience into an experience to increase their emotional involvement. By surrounding them with sights, sounds, tastes, smells, and tactile stimuli, you fully engage them. You may not have a 3-D helmet for each member; however, consider what you can do to create a sensory experience.

HANDS-ON PRACTICE

Your audience can learn how your solution works, feels, or responds if you give them time to practice with it. This component significantly boosts their understanding, preference, and desire to purchase or use it. Plus, it increases their memory about the points you make. For example, the opportunity to practice with woodworking tools or a software program may help the audience see how much more quickly or expertly they can perform their tasks.

QUESTIONS AND ANSWERS

Rather than wait for the end of your presentation to engage the audience with questions and answers, set aside some time during your content delivery to have that dialogue. When you ask for questions, you might need to have some frequently asked questions ready, so the audience members can "warm up" or get the courage to jump in.

Role-play

Putting your audience to work in small groups can help them experience their deficits, creativity, abilities, or increasing level of mastery upon instruction. When you role-play in two phases, the need for your guidance or product is clear. Phase one would be without the aids they need, so a sense of self-doubt or frustration strikes them. Then, phase two would be with some of the support you provide, so they feel how beneficial your solution would be for them.

TIPS

Tips are bite-sized, easy to follow, and often intriguing "hacks." Take complex matters and reduce them down to a list or set of instructions that activate "can-do" thinking. Communicate "you got this."

Content components associated with tips you might have in your Library of Success include:

1. Advanced Techniques, Shortcuts, or Hacks
2. Lists of Do's and Don'ts
3. Step-by-Step Instructions
4. Tips, Hints, and Prompts

DESCRIPTIONS

Advanced Techniques, Shortcuts, or Hacks

Sharing high-level finesse or know-how you gained from experience or in-depth study is a powerful way to accelerate the feeling of mastery in an audience. Teaching an advanced technique may take practice on your part so the steps are easy to mimic or pick up and you aren't merely engaged in a daunting display of your prowess. When it's possible, reduce the process down to a shortcut or hack. That often means showing what to do and not explaining the background about how you came up with the technique.

Lists of Do's and Don'ts

When you want to communicate best practices in a simple format, compile a list of "should's and should not's." This component gives you the opportunity to point out minefields your audience should fear and gives them a checklist of what works. Overall, a list of "do's and don'ts" inspire confidence they can rely on your guidance about a spectrum of related issues.

STEP-BY-STEP INSTRUCTIONS

Easy to follow instructions provide clear and organized directions about how to execute a task. Think about following a recipe for making a cake and how vital it is to do things in precisely the right order. A cake won't bake and a soufflé will fall unless you follow step-by-step instructions. Whether you are delegating assignments to colleagues or releasing a new product, providing step-by-step instructions makes even a complex task approachable and straightforward. Errors are reduced. This component makes an audience optimistic they can succeed without stress.

TIPS, HINTS OR PROMPTS

Passing along your knowledge of useful "tricks of the trade" can make a project seem easier or faster to complete. When collaborating in a team, sharing good advice and providing friendly or structured guidance is imperative for creating a nourishing and inclusive environment. Knowing you are prepared to help them succeed increases your audience's perception that you are trustworthy and supportive.

ACCOUNTABILITY

Accountability includes documentation that details how and why you and your audience are moving forward together. Make sure you choose content components that are appropriate for the link you are in. When it's the right time to go over financial and legal issues or agreements, lead the communication with the same clarity, sincerity, and trustworthiness that have defined your approach to collaboration throughout your presentation.

Content components associated with accountability you might have in your Library of Success include:

1. Budgets
2. Contracts
3. Forecasts
4. Letters of Agreement
5. Roadmaps and Timelines
6. Specifications
7. Total Cost and Use Analyses

DESCRIPTIONS

BUDGETS

A budget is an estimate or plan that outlines an organization's anticipated income and expenses for a specific time period. You may find the term budget used to describe a line item expense projection or simply the total amount of money allocated to a project. If you expect that funds have already been identified or allocated, inquire about the size of a budget. You might be asked to create a budget for your solution, which would prompt you to ask if they want a breakdown of costs or simply a total cost. Lastly, consider that funds earmarked for other expenses could be reallocated to your project, if no budget or funds are otherwise available.

CONTRACTS

A contract is a legally binding agreement between two or more parties that contains an exchange of promises. Contracts can be oral, written, or implied, although written agreements will be easier to enforce. Not all contracts are written to be adjudicated in a court of law should the parties disagree on whether the terms were met. You may decide to use arbitration or almost any other mechanism to determine who prevails in case of a conflict.

FORECAST

A forecast is a prediction of expected future trends, such as a sales forecast. It's typically done by examining and analyzing existing data, historical patterns, and predictions about factors that might impact performance. It is a projection that often displays facts, figures, and statistics in such layouts as graphs, charts, and tables. A company can use a forecast to determine its future objectives by looking at past performance, changes within the organization, and market opportunities.

LETTERS OF AGREEMENT

An agreement lays out the principles of a working relationship or obligation between parties. You may outline when you will deliver the product or work, how often meetings or calls will take place, costs, payment schedules, and other details that make it possible to commence work or formally begin a working relationship.

Roadmaps and Timelines

These are organizational tools that allow a company to sequence events and subsequently track their progress. Typically laid out in a chart or graph, they display the different stages or activities involved in a project, along with expected dates of completion. Roadmaps and timelines help guide a company throughout a plan, keeping everyone on task, and finishing their part on time.

Specifications

Sometimes called a "spec," specifications form a detailed description of a product or service. It is often used to put out a request for bids or to assure a company that its vendors fully understand a company's requirements. Frequently, specifications can be negotiated, for example, when the company's demands are at odds with what a vendor is willing to deliver.

Total Cost and Use Analyses

It may be surprising, but purchase price is only one factor in calculating the total cost of a good or service. This concept is particularly important when a competitor appears to be less expensive, or you face resistance about price. Here's a good equation for this concept.

Acquisition Costs + Possession Costs + Usage Costs = Total Cost and Use

Given all contributing factors, your solution may be the best value, even if your purchase price is higher. For example, you provide greater value if you supply low-cost financing, free installation, or a year of free training and support. Other than price, consider how these factors reduce the total expense. 1) The cost of transportation or set up. 2) Costs of acquiring and managing products or services, such as stocking shelves and keeping inventory on hand. 3) The durability of the product or service over its complete life cycle, including the need for repairs or spare parts. 4) The cost of insurance, which may go up or down given how your product or service impacts the potential liability your customer faces in their business. 5) The reduction or elimination of personnel or travel expenses.

CONGRATULATIONS!

You made it past the second major milestone of the Speak Up System! We've covered all the segments in Act Two, your Streamlined Content. You've heard how to use content to achieve the "know-like-ignite" stages of the transformation channel.

ONWARD!

Now you're ready to dig deeper into the strategy and tactics of the Speak Up System Act Three: your Great Closing. Onward to this last and crucial stage of the Transformation Channel: getting action and commitments.

Section Ten

Act 3, Segment 1 (Recall Promises Kept)

WHAT'S IN THIS SECTION?

Chapter 23: Recall Promises Kept

ACT 1: GREAT OPENING
Segment 1: Introduce Yourself
Segment 2: Introduce Topic
Segment 3: Make Promises
ACT 2: STREAMLINED CONTENT
Segment 1: Foster Understanding
Segment 2: Create Belief
Segment 3: Ignite Urgency
ACT 3: GREAT CLOSING
Segment 1: Recall Promises Kept
Segment 2: Add Unexpected Value
Segment 3: Give Instructions

Section Ten
Key Concepts

AT THIS POINT IN YOUR PRESENTATION, YOUR AUDIENCE ENTERS THE LAST stage of the Transformation Channel. You guide them to take action as you planned. Mutual gain, that is, achieving your outcome and benefiting your audience, is the job of Act Three, your Great Closing.

In the first segment of Act Three, you deepen your relationship with the audience by recalling promises you made and kept during your presentation. That intensifies how much they trust, like, and care about you. The ideal refrain in your audience's brain is: "Wow! You did exactly what you said you would!"

This segment also reinforces: 1) what they now understand about the topic, 2) why they believe your solution or approach is best, and 3) how urgent it is to move forward with you now.

The strategy for this segment is simple. You repeat the promises you made in Act One, your Great Opening. Then you highlight the relevant content you shared that fulfilled your promises during Act Two, your Streamlined Content.

Section Ten
CHAPTER 23

Recall Promises Kept

Great Closing, Segment One (Recall Promises Kept)

RELATIONSHIPS ARE THE FRUIT THAT BLOSSOMS FROM MAKING AND keeping promises. Thus, before you harvest your bounty from this relationship, you draw the audience's attention to: 1) what you promised at the onset of your presentation, and 2) what you accomplished during it.

One of these phrases may be perfect to launch your closing:

1. As I promised you when we began this presentation, you now can …
2. My commitment to you today was that you would receive …
3. During our meeting today, I started off with the guarantee that you will …
4. Let's see if you got what I promised!

HIT THE HIGHLIGHTS

Take the fastest and clearest route through this segment. Don't deliver your presentation again. Just use names for the content components you shared or substitute in quick headlines about them. Keep it short and don't reference any component that took your audience above or beyond what you promised.

For example, you might identify a specific promise and note that you fulfilled it by providing your audience with:

- Our product's invention story
- Testimonials
- Our role-play
- A product demonstration
- The video
- Step-by-step instructions
- Comparison of alternative courses of action
- The risk analysis
- Roadmaps and timelines

SUCCEED THROUGH SPEED

By using the term rather than rehashing the details, you speed up players' recollections, instantly amplify their feelings of fulfillment as well as anchor in their respect and regard for you.

REINFORCEMENT THROUGH REPETITION

Whenever possible, use the exact same words or phrases you used in Act One and Act Two. Now is not the time to introduce new information or terms. In this segment, you are reinforcing one point: you make and keep promises. Do not distract, confuse, or do anything to take away from the fact that you are as good as your words.

Here are examples that show how speakers connect their Great Opening Segment Three: make promises, with their Great Closing Segment One: recall promises kept.

EXAMPLE #1: BRIEFING-STYLE MEETING

Call center supervisor Ken MacDonald is seeking clear-cut authority to implement his proposed changes without further collaboration with other employees or a review by outside consultants.

In his Great Opening Segment Three: make promises, Ken said:

"At the conclusion of this briefing, you may make a 33% improvement in our call center's productivity by authorizing a limited set of actions. I promise you'll be pleased to discover most measures require no funding. Plus, the new program delivers a very attractive and proven ROI."

Now, in his Great Closing Segment One: recall promises kept, Ken says:

"At the commencement of this briefing, I promised that through a limited set of actions you could make a 33% improvement in our call center productivity. The success stories, new industry standards, expert analysis, and recommendations set out exactly how to get that jump in productivity. I also promised these actions would require low or no funding, and thus deliver a very attractive ROI. As you saw from the total cost of purchase and use analysis, forecast, and roadmap, my recommendations deliver exactly that ROI."

EXAMPLE #2: PERSUASIVE-STYLE MEETING

Technical sales representative Lynn Finerman is selling testing and measurement equipment and upgrades to a prospect in their third linked interaction. Her outcome is to secure the first order.

In her Great Opening Segment Three: make promises, Lynn said:

"The information I'll reveal today will help you avoid the most devastating consequences of poor steam quality. You'll see why the legacy system that is failing in over 70% of cogeneration plants today will soon be replaced industry-wide. By using the industry's new diagnostic form to assess your system, I guarantee you'll leave this meeting with complete confidence you can fix your quality problem with the right-sized solution."

Now, in her Great Closing Segment One: recall promises kept, Lynn says:

"During my introduction, I promised to reveal the most devastating consequences of poor steam quality. You saw exactly that in the case histories' data and analysis. I also promised you would see why the system is failing in over 70% of cogeneration plants. In the industry-wide evaluation, the experts were clear about the cause. Finally, I guaranteed you would leave this meeting with complete confidence you have the right-sized solution for your problem. The assessment and forecast you just completed give you that confidence."

EXAMPLE #3: TEAM-STYLE MEETING

Jack Hansen wants his staff to deliver the finished storyboard for the client's infomercial and keep its production schedule on time, and on target with the objectives and budget.

In his Great Opening Segment Three: make promises, Jack said:

"I promise this meeting will pay off by giving you the exact results you desire from this project. Together, we will reframe the work plan, so it accurately reflects the time and support you need to accomplish your work. You'll have the opportunity to talk about the obstacles facing you, and we'll identify the resources or exchange information to overcome those obstacles. Before we leave, you'll approve a roadmap that guarantees you get what you need so you can perform your job with minimum stress and maximum speed."

Then, in his Great Closing Segment One: recall promises kept, Jack says:

"This morning, I kicked off the meeting with three promises. First promise: you would get exactly the results you desire from this project. From our rewards and results session, it's crystal clear this project delivers those results and is worth moving to the top of our list at full-speed ahead. Second promise: a forum to identify the obstacles facing you, and the resources and information you need to overcome those obstacles. Your assessments and questionnaires revealed those. My third promise: a roadmap that not only sets out your deliverables but also schedules the time and materials you need at each juncture of the project.

Thanks to a great communication facilitation by our project manager, here's our newly completed roadmap that minimizes stress and maximizes speed."

EXAMPLE #4: TRAINING-STYLE MEETING

IT database manager Gary Singleton wants sales reps to learn how to use a new database to generate high-quality leads and stop bothering administrative support staff to do it for them.

In his Great Opening Segment Three: make promises, Gary said:

"Today you'll tap into the database and discover a fast and easy way to increase and accelerate your revenue production. I promise by the time we conclude today, you'll have a list of customers in your territory who are ready to purchase upgrades and who will welcome your call. I also guarantee you'll locate at least three strong new prospects with a connection to your current accounts—they're in sister companies. You'll become a master at generating the most profitable leads and be able to meet and exceed your quota."

Then, in his Great Closing Segment One: recall promises kept, Gary says:

"When we began this training, I promised a fast and easy way to increase and accelerate your revenue production. You got that as soon as you saw the system demonstration. I also promised you would have a list of customers who would welcome your call because they are ready to purchase upgrades. By using your own territory's data in the hands-on practice, you created a list you can start calling this very afternoon. I also guaranteed three strong prospects just from using the links to your current accounts. By using the step-by-step instructions, that's what you netted. Finally, I gave you my word you will become a master at generating leads that result in your meeting and exceeding quota. With the advanced techniques supplied in your handout, you are ready to do just that."

ONWARD!

You have just two segments to go in the SPEAK UP SYSTEM!

Section Eleven

Act 2, Segment 3 (Add Unexpected Value)

WHAT'S IN THIS SECTION?

Chapter 24: Tangible Gifts

Chapter 25: Intangible Gifts

ACT 1: GREAT OPENING
  Segment 1: Introduce Yourself
  Segment 2: Introduce Topic
  Segment 3: Make Promises
ACT 2: STREAMLINED CONTENT
  Segment 1: Foster Understanding
  Segment 2: Create Belief
  Segment 3: Ignite Urgency
ACT 3: GREAT CLOSING
  Segment 1: Recall Promises Kept
  Segment 2: Add Unexpected Value
  Segment 3: Give Instructions

Section Eleven
Key Concepts

You are about to surprise your audience by exceeding their expectations for the presentation. Your ideal outcome is this refrain in your audience's brain: "Wow! You are over-delivering on your promises!"

Your unexpected gift at this moment amplifies their feeling of urgency to act because it goes beyond the incentive you offered in Act Two. Your "sweetener" could double or triple the value of their taking action, by increasing the actual monetary benefits of your solution. Alternatively, a gift at this time may be only symbolic, memorializing your genuine interest, respect, and compassion for them. In either case, you are about to supersize their satisfaction with you and your presentation.

Your goal is to tip the relationship out of balance, creating "reciprocity anxiety." That happens when the audience is deeply in your debt. Most people subconsciously seek to balance the "relationship scale," by cooperating with the person who provides an abundance of value. You will give them that opportunity via your instructions in the final segment of your Great Closing.

Section Eleven
CHAPTER 24

Tangible Gifts

Alternative #1 for a Great Closing, Segment Two (Add Unexpected Value)

T HE FIRST WAY TO DELIVER UNEXPECTED VALUE IS BY OFFERING A TANGIBLE
gift, helping your audience to think: "Wow! You are over-delivering on
your promises!"

THINK LOW COST, HIGH VALUE

Surprise the audience with a valuable token or reward, such as a gift card or
pen. Even something symbolic significantly increases their satisfaction. A
memento deepens their emotional connection to you now and in the future.
A certificate, badge, trophy,, and online recognition are also tangible and often
low-cost gifts, with high value because they are visible to others.

INTELLECTUAL PROPERTY

Frequently you can offer something your audience prizes but costs you nothing
or next to it to produce. These gifts include reports, charts, comparisons,
preview copies of specifications, digital media such as podcasts, e-content, or
even VIP tours of your plant.

EXAMPLE #1

When I train executives in business development, I typically make this type
of offer in Segment Two of my Great Closing. I say:

"Now, I'd like to offer you something more: a gift from me to you. You know
some of my professional coaching is with celebrities, high-level executives, and
high net worth individuals. Specifically, I coach them in the field of personal
reputation or what we now call personal branding. I want you to be super
successful in your field and get the most value from every connection you
make. Would you like a copy of my new book, *Billion Dollar Personal Branding*?"

EXAMPLE #2

Reiko is a sales representative for a company that customizes home closets. Initially, her company's training department provided a color wheel to help her sketch out attractive designs as she pitched prospects on different facings, trim, knobs, and other closet options. On her first-ever sales appointment, Reiko brought out the color wheel to create a closet design for a woman she'll never forget and always appreciate, Katie Sossner.

After Reiko created the design, Katie asked if she could buy a color wheel for her own use. She said it gave her ideas for new ways to mix and match her wardrobe. When Reiko offered to give her the color wheel, Katie didn't need another minute to sign the contract and get her closet project started immediately. Hence, Reiko's first call on a prospect became her first sale to a customer. She now uses the color wheel as unexpected added value.

Here's how Reiko used the experience to create a winning Great Closing Segment Two. She now says:

"I'd like to offer you this color wheel. Use it, and you'll see how to make the most out of the clothes you have in your wardrobe, perhaps mixing and matching some combinations you never would have thought of otherwise. Once your closet is installed, you can hang coordinated clothes together. Every morning you'll get dressed in a jiffy and look great. Plus, you'll enjoy how simply elegant this closet system will look and how easy it will be to use once we install it. Would you like the wheel?"

EXAMPLE #3

Ride is a small urban-oriented ad agency. When Ride executives pitch new clients, they deliver a presentation with great music. The firm takes the music as a trade from the artists they represent. That music is one of Ride's assets.

When Ride executives come to their Great Closing Segment Two, they offer a download by saying:

"Seeing how much you enjoyed the music behind our presentation, I'd like to offer you something that's outside our business goals for you, but that I think will get you pumped up at the gym or get your house rocking if you throw a party. We commissioned this music for our presentation, but would you like to download it for your own use?"

SWEETENERS

Remember Mary Poppins famously offering a spoonful of sugar to make the medicine go down? You may add a similar sweetener to move an audience to take action as they exit your interaction. For this purpose, gift certificates and gift cards may be in small denominations, yet still hold significant value.

EXAMPLE #4

At a trade show presentation, engineer Todd Lilaw offers a gift certificate to set up the next link in his relationship map. He needs players to exit his seminar and happily engage in conversation with the sales representatives waiting nearby.

In his Great Closing Segment Two and Three, Todd says:

"Would you like to receive a gift certificate you can use when you need a break from the hustle and bustle of this trade show? Please proceed to the pod where you see all the green gift bags. You may pick up your package and gift certificate there."

GIFTS ARE SYMBOLS

Tangible gifts are valuable, but they are also symbolic. They represent your intention, values, and desire to be involved in an ongoing relationship with your audience. Consider what reflects well on you and has value to your audience. This might be samples, materials, premiums, books, food, or anything else your audience can take away from your interaction. It extends their memory of you.

Companies that are known for collectibles, including The Coca-Cola Company, often produce a commemorative pin or another limited-edition item. The memento is symbolic of what the brand represents. A limited-edition collectible offers a special connection with a prestige brand. Of course, your audience may also turn that collectible into cash on an Internet auction site. You can invent, customize, or select a gift by shopping with premium companies and incentive firms.

EXPENSIVE GIFTS

There are only a few conditions that are appropriate for an expensive gift.

EXAMPLE #5

Equipment sales representative Tony Michaels' gateway outcome is to collect the signed sales contract and get a start date for installation.

In his Great Closing Segment Two, Tony says:

"When we come together next week to set up installation dates, I'll look forward to collecting the contract and seeing the CEO's sign-off on the roadmap and timeline. Now, I would like to offer you this beautiful pen as a memento of that action. This pen commemorates the beginning of the results and rewards your company will enjoy soon after installation. May I give you this pen?"

USEFUL GIFTS

Giving something that improves how your audience performs at work raises their satisfaction and keeps you top of mind.

EXAMPLE #6

At a trade show, Jim Mariz offers a tangible gift that improves how his audience does their job when they return to work. Here is how he uses that gift to get people walking to the back of the room where they interact with his staff to make appointments.

In his Great Closing Segment Two, Jim says:

"I want to offer you a kit that has amazed many plant managers. It has the tools, along with the worksheets, you need to assess your plant. However, if you are already sleeping well at night because your plant faces no danger of a sudden, unplanned shutdown, then don't bother with the kit. You are doing great—don't mess with success."

NOT TOO MUCH

In Great Closing Segment Two, don't offer such a fabulous gift that it distracts your audience or makes players uncomfortable. An over-the-top gift risks dragging you off your path to success. Consider this analogy. In your social life, it's nice to bring flowers when you are a guest at a dinner party. However, don't purchase a set of dining chairs! That would be too much.

Use the Goldilocks Principle. Don't offer anything too big or too small. Go for something that is "just right."

RULES TO KEEP IN MIND

Gifts are not bribes. Be mindful of your company's culture and policies. Your unexpected added value is merely a mechanism to increase your audience's satisfaction ROI. You want them to feel an irresistible pull to reciprocate, which is why you give instructions immediately after Segment Two.

Now, let's consider another type of unexpected added value: intangible gifts.

Section Eleven
CHAPTER 25

Intangible Gifts
Alternative #2 for a Great Closing, Segment Two (Add Unexpected Value)

A NOTHER WAY TO DELIVER UNEXPECTED VALUE IS BY OFFERING AN intangible gift. You may delight your audience, help them have fun, or congratulate them. As you select the right gift, make sure it reflects the nature of your relationship.

PLAYFUL ENGAGEMENT

Delight the audience with a fun way to interact with your content. For example, you might introduce a game, contest, drawing, or sweepstakes that incents them to complete or submit assessments or use your training. You can structure this experience so everyone wins a small prize. Alternatively, rewards can be limited, depending on what suits your goals.

Intangible gifts are engaging because they represent an opportunity rather than the value of the actual item. By analogy, when you play the lottery, you get a receipt to hold on to, but you didn't put down your cash because you wanted that small piece of paper. You purchased a chance to win a large sum of money. To the people operating the lottery and promoting the prize, you are saying: "Wow, I want exactly what you're offering!" Plus, there's the fun factor of taking a chance to win.

GAMES

If you only have one interaction on your relationship map, a game is an excellent choice for making your content and the mindset transformation "stick." Games increase involvement or emotional connection. In general, while engaged in a game, the harder the player works to win points or create entries, the more likely it is they will win. Set up rules that reward performance.

RULES FOR GAMES

Along with meeting the requirements of the law and your own company's policies, games must be appropriate for the relationship and the players. You may offer:

1. Several attractive prizes so all the players are excited by the favorable odds of winning something valuable.
2. A variety of ways to win, so each player is encouraged by a reward that relates to a strength or advantage they have.

You must provide:

1. Clear rules or guidelines for how to win.
2. Absolute honesty and transparency about the award of prizes.

OUT OF SIGHT, BUT TOP OF MIND

Pump up awareness by promoting your game outside of the interaction, when that is feasible. Use posters, email, and talk it up in conversation. If the game will take place over many weeks or months, provide a website or chart where you or the players post results at regular intervals, perhaps on a daily or weekly basis. You may have interim prizes at certain milestones, along with a grand prize at the end.

EXAMPLE #1

On link four of his relationship map, sales representative Tony Michaels facilitates a training-style meeting with his prospective system users. Tony needs users to follow up, after this interaction. Specifically, he needs them to trial his software when they get back to their desks.

In his Great Closing Segment Two, Tony says:

"I want to offer you a challenge, a chance to see how you rank against all of our software users. Depending on your skill, you can win some great prizes. You'll find the rules and the prizes on our company's website by logging on with the passcodes you'll receive before you leave today. The challenge is this. It takes the average user 20 minutes to master the protocol in our package. If you can match that time, you win a free subscription to one of many cool magazines listed on the prize page. Plus, if you can beat it, you get to pick from a fantastic group of electronic gadgets. You'll see those on the prize page, too. You just need to log in. The software trial will start up onscreen with prompts that take you through it. Just remember, the clock starts as soon as you make your first keystroke. Would you like to compete with our other users and win some prizes?"

CONGRATULATING WINNERS, EMBRACING LOSERS

Sometimes it's appropriate to boost the profile of the winners. For example, sales managers typically hold a steak and hamburger dinner. The contest winners enjoy steak, while the losers eat hamburger.

At other times, it's inappropriate to create such a stark contrast between winning and losing. For example, crew members may not have equal mental or physical skills. In that case, reward the winners, but make sure everyone gets a prize of some kind. Participation awards like a pair of movie tickets help avoid sinking morale among the lackluster performers.

Be careful not to set up rivalries that lead to conflict in the workplace.

EXAMPLE #2

Apparel chain store owner Harry Harounian is instituting rules to keep merchandise out of the dressing rooms and rapidly returned to the sales floor fixtures. Harry holds a pizza and soft drink party for all the clerks after this meeting, as a morale builder. The party is a small, shared prize that rewards everyone for attending the meeting.

In Segment Two of a team-style interaction with store clerks, Harry says:

"I would like to offer you something more. Beginning tomorrow morning, you get the opportunity to win even better prizes. We're implementing a mystery shopper program for the next four weeks. On all shifts, evaluators who appear to be customers will visit the store, watching to see which clerks use the new 'rapid clean up' system effectively. Plus, store management will be on the lookout as well. If a mystery shopper or manager catches you 'doing it right,' meaning you are using the clean-up and re-rack system efficiently, you'll be awarded ten points on the spot. At the end of the month, the top five individuals and top three teams with the most points win prizes. You can see on this board what team you're on, so you can coach each other and increase your chances of winning. Are you ready to win this contest?"

EXAMPLE #3

Before leaving the interaction, a trainer wants her audience to complete and turn in evaluation forms.

In her Great Closing Segment Two, she says:

"As we discussed, part of managing stress is healthy eating. I have an opportunity for six people in this room to win a free lunch at the sandwich restaurant in our office park. Does a free lunch sound good right now? Also, remember to make it a healthy sandwich or salad."

Then in her Great Closing Segment Three, she gives these instructions.

"Complete the evaluation form in your packet. It will take three minutes. When you're done, fold your paper in half, from top to bottom. When everyone has dropped a form into the bowl, I'll close my eyes and pick six forms out of it. Those lucky six win a free lunch. Let me entice you by waving these restaurant coupons. Now ready, set, evaluate!"

TESTS AND ASSESSMENTS

Tests are a measurement tool most often associated with training meetings. However, you may provide pre- and post- content assessments in any interaction style. Players may complete the test and privately evaluate their progress, or you may administer the tests and evaluate the results.

EXAMPLE #4

In this example, senior IT trainer Jennifer Lipton is training new IT technicians.

In her Great Closing Segment One, she says:

"I promised you'd start off on the right foot, and now you know from the hands-on practice and troubleshooting guide that you're using a lot more than that foot around here! You know how to run your complete workstation and interact successfully with the system."

In her Great Closing Segment Two, Jennifer says:

"I have an opportunity for you to see just how far you've come in your mastery of this material. Would you like to see how much stronger, faster, and smarter you are now?"

Finally, in her Great Closing Segment Three, Jennifer says:

"Here is an assessment that helps you measure exactly how far you've come. There's a question or brief exercise for each component we covered. Take the next ten minutes to complete the assessment. Then, we'll have a quick debrief to go over the answers just before you leave. I'll also provide these advanced techniques and some interesting examples for you to look at if you finish early. So, pencils up. Here's the assessment. Pencils down and go!"

APPLAUSE, APPLAUSE

You may invite self-reporting as a sweetener with an assessment. When players report their results, articulate your approval or direct the group to show its appreciation to each participant. You may instruct the audience to applaud or provide some other acknowledgment.

EXAMPLE #5

Consultant Serena Bazin uses this Great Closing in her presentation on the "Do's and Don'ts of Business Relationships."

In her Great Closing Segment Two, Serena says:

"Now I'd like to offer you the opportunity to share your findings from the role-play you did with your team. After each person contributes, I'd like to reward his or her participation with a round of applause. Are you ready to be appreciated?"

ONWARD!

The next segment is a giant step to success: you give instructions and get action.

Section Twelve

Act 3, Segment 3 (Give Instructions)

WHAT'S IN THIS SECTION?

Chapter 26: Action & Commitments

ACT 1: GREAT OPENING
Segment 1: Introduce Yourself
Segment 2: Introduce Topic
Segment 3: Make Promises
ACT 2: STREAMLINED CONTENT
Segment 1: Foster Understanding
Segment 2: Create Belief
Segment 3: Ignite Urgency
ACT 3: GREAT CLOSING
Segment 1: Recall Promises Kept
Segment 2: Add Unexpected Value
Segment 3: Give Instructions

Section Twelve
Key Concepts

NOW YOU SEE YOUR OUTCOME COME TO FRUITION. IN THIS SEGMENT, YOU help your audience get through the very last, mission-critical stage of the Transformation Channel: taking action and making future commitments. The ideal refrain in your audience's brain is: "Wow! I am moving forward on my goals!"

Often, Segment Three is a short and gratifying time for your audience and you. It's the culmination of mutual gain. You are fulfilling their goals and your proximate outcome.

There is no hard sell and no resistance—because your presentation created the necessary transformation in your audience's hearts and minds. You also just magnified their desire to take action, by providing unexpected added value right before you tell them what to do now.

Keep your instructions simple and clear: they should be part of your rehearsed trigger talk. Have everything your audience needs to take action: pens, forms, online access, and calendar plus whatever you offered as your unexpected added value (if that's appropriate). If you also need commitments for a next action or interaction, be ready with additional instructions that are easy to follow.

Section Twelve
Chapter 26

Action & Commitments
Great Closing, Segment Three (Give Instructions)

THIS LAST SEGMENT IS SIMPLE. GIVE INSTRUCTIONS AND GET THE RESULTS you planned for this interaction. Depending on its link on your relationship map, this presentation could get you your proximate outcome, gateway outcome, and relationship outcome!

GET WHAT YOU WANT

Once you give instructions, stop talking so everyone can follow them. Don't do or say anything to distract players from immediately taking action. You don't want them to feel you might have something more to share. Any hesitation you cause in this final segment will delay or possibly even deny you the outcome you've been driving toward.

TRIGGER TALK TIME

Have your instructions firmly ingrained in your brain, so you confidently instruct your audience precisely what to do at this point in your presentation. This is a crucial time to have trigger talk so that you can be clear, concise, and specific. You may be giving instructions about how to complete a contract, write a check, craft their offer letter to you, or anything else you planned to culminate your presentation.

The action should feel natural and satisfying for both you and your audience. You have everything you need from them: they trust you, like you, and care about you. They have everything they need from you: information, support for their decision-making, a sense of urgency, incentives, and added value. The relationship scale is tipped heavily in your favor. They are ready to reciprocate.

KEY POINTS

1. To increase compliance, use the word couplet "would-because."
2. Repeat your instructions twice to fix your plan in the minds of your audience.
3. Stop talking and allow time for everyone to complete the task you set for them.
4. Finish your Great Closing with an enthusiastic PAW like "Great!" or "Well done!"
5. Be prepared with everything that will assist your audience in taking action with ease.
6. Be prepared to pack up elegantly and swiftly.
7. Briefly answer last-minute questions from individuals and say your good-byes.

THE POWER COUPLET: WOULD-BECAUSE

Consider adding "would-because" to your instructions, when you sense any hesitation from your players at the end of Segment Two. That word combination has almost magical powers when it comes to guiding a player to make a decision and take immediate action. For example, you could say, "Go to the back of the room to sign up for your installation." However, you will get a better response if you say, "Would you go to the back of the room to sign up for your installation because the list we take home today will get priority treatment."

You may find these words useful in sparking your own trigger talk for Segment Three. You might say:

- "Would you click on the right-hand side of the Web page and voila! You see the prizes and the rules for how you can win them because the contest starts today."
- "Would you sign the form at the bottom of the page, and then we'll call your loading dock to tell them the truck is pulling up because the dock might close."
- "Would you simply open your calendar—whether it's on paper or in your hand-held device—and on the page or spot for March 14, enter the words 'advanced training,' because you don't want to miss that opportunity."
- "Would you like to pick up the phone and call the agency right now, while we're all here together because this detail might get lost in our rush to get out the campaign."

- "Would you write out the check for one hundred and eighty-six thousand, four hundred and thirty-eight dollars. That's 1-8-6 comma 4-3-8 because that deposit kicks off the development cycle."
- "Would you send me a copy of that email now because that way you'll get a response more quickly."

REPETITION

Repeat your instructions twice, if possible. The repetition helps to plant your plan into players' brains. Here are your options:

1. Use the same words in both instances
2. Change the order of the words
3. Modify your phrasing using different words

EXAMPLE #1

To see repetition in action, once again let's focus on a trade show presentation, which is link one on a software sales relationship map.

In his Great Closing Segment Two, add unexpected value, Todd LiLaw announces:

"I'd like to offer you a package to take back to your office. In it, you'll find our software demonstration plus a gift certificate you may redeem at several retailers or their online stores. It's our gesture of appreciation for your interest. Would you like to have those packages now?"

Then, in his closing Segment Three, give instructions, he says:

"Let's do that! Please proceed to the pod where you see all the green gift bags. You may pick up your package and gift certificate there."

As you can see in this example, the first time Todd says: "...proceed to the pod where you see all the green gift bags." The second time, he says: "...pick up your package and gift certificate there."

PATIENCE AND COMPASSION BEFORE MOVING ON

Quietly wait and watch them while they complete the action you instructed them to take. See if they need help. Be compassionate and respectful if you offer to assist them. Once they've taken action, begin speaking about the next step.

For example, you may want to give instructions for any follow-up action or commitment you desire. You might remind your players to review handouts, or pass them on to subordinates, superiors, and trusted advisors, or hold their own interactions before you see them again.

EXAMPLE #2

In her Great Closing Segment Three, a group vice-president speaking to department heads watches them follow her instructions. Then to direct their next step, she says:

"Great! Here is the next step. Take this handout back to your desk. You will also find an electronic copy of it in your email. Would you forward that email to your entire team, because they need this information as well. You may make hard copies and distribute it that way, or you may forward the electronic copy that is in your email inbox. So, your follow-up action is to share the handout with your team because they need it to prepare for our next meeting."

SAY GOOD-BYE

Watch them prepare to follow up. They may be making notes or putting dates on their calendar. Then, answer any questions and respond to their feedback, being as brief as possible. You don't want to launch another interaction. You want to stay in control of the outcome.

Share your farewells and whatever other pleasantries you find appropriate. Ideally, you have those phrases on a trigger, so your words flow naturally and calmly. It's harder than you might imagine containing your surprise when everything goes precisely as you planned! Rehearse.

Be prepared to neatly put away whatever materials you have. Bring carrying cases or boxes. Shut down electronics and tidy up the area, if that's your responsibility. Then, make your exit.

DO'S AND DON'TS

Don't automatically say "thank you" at the end of Segment Three. Your audience is taking action because they believe it is in their best interest. The refrain in their brain is something close to: "Wow, this was a tremendous value of my time and attention! I'm delighted to do this. I'm glad I didn't miss out."

Given that mindset, your "thank you" could pull them back toward resistance. You could trigger a player to think: "I'm getting the benefits, so why are you thanking me? Is there something going on here that's not all about satisfying me?"

HOW TO RESPOND TO THEIR ACTION AND COMMITMENTS

As a communication leader, acknowledge them for taking action. For example, you might affirm them by giving a PAW, such as:

- Great work!
- Well done!
- Super!
- Brilliant!
- Excellent!
- Great to work with you!
- Great to talk to you!
- Nice to meet you!
- Congratulations!
- Here's to your success!

RESPONDING TO COMPLIMENTS

Even when you get a direct compliment, think twice before you say: "thank you." When an audience member tells me, "Wow, you're a very motivating speaker," I don't typically react to it as a compliment. Instead, I respond to the comment by sharing the credit, because I see what I do as part of a collaboration with my audience. Therefore, I reflect on the audience's positive characteristics. I might say:

"This is a great group—so much achievement and commitment. It is great to be here, applying these concepts."

You might also be ready to respond to a compliment you receive regarding your powerful speaking skills. You could reflect on the collaboration that took place under your communication leadership by saying:

"My company invests a lot of training in our employees. We receive the skill building and tools we need to communicate professionally. Our goal is to be the best ambassadors possible, not only for our company but also for our industry. It was great to get to do that with you today."

TIPS FOR GETTING PLAYERS TO TAKE ACTION AS YOU DESIRE

1. Flow naturally from your closing Segment Two. Don't introduce an abrupt change of tone.
2. Frame simple instructions, making it clear how they can get the added value you described in Segment Two.

3. Put everything your audience needs in front of them—documents, tools, or devices —anything that will result in their ability to take action or make commitments to follow up as you desire.

TAKE RESPONSIBILITY FOR THEIR EXPERIENCE

You are room parent, teacher, managing partner, fearless leader, and tribal elder at this point. Before you speak up, consider your desired outcome and the action that demonstrates it. Then, gather what you need and what the audience needs, so the action flows seamlessly. For example, if you are:

- Registering them via computer: have one powered up
- Directing them to sign a contract: have a working pen
- Making appointments: have your schedule open
- Asking for business cards: have a place to put them
- Taking cash: have change
- Accepting electronic payments: have the right device or site up
- Assessing their performance: have an answer key
- Recording their progress: have a way to log it
- Delivering bad news: have tissues

Now that you have all the rules and steps to help you construct a Great Closing, these examples will help spark your own Great Closings. Let's revisit some examples of closing segments from previous chapters and add some new ones.

EXAMPLE #3

Here is Jim Mariz making a presentation to plant managers at a trade show.

In his Great Closing Segment One, recall promises kept, Jim says:

"As I promised when we first came together for this presentation, you now have the procedures for testing and diagnosing each component of your system. You have seen the new formula for risk estimation the leading expert in our industry devised and personally uses. You know it works if you believe the testimonials and applications shared by the three large-scale operators and the more than twenty companies of all sizes who have reported their results and rewards."

In his Great Closing Segment Two, add more unexpected value, Jim says:

"I want to offer you a kit that has amazed many plant managers. It has the tools, along with the worksheets, you need to assess your plant. However, if you are already sleeping well at night because your plant faces no danger of a sudden, unplanned shutdown, then don't bother with the kit. You are doing great—don't mess with success."

In his Great Closing Segment Three, give instructions, Jim says:

"However, if you do want to evaluate your components, I have a limited number of these kits with me that you can take with you right now. The only thing I ask in return is that when you sign out a kit, you take the one made for your system configuration. They are numbered so if you lose one, we'll know exactly what batch it came from, and we can replace it quickly and at no cost to you. So, keep the kit and the tools. Just make sure you get the right kit when you sign them out as you leave. At a later date, I will follow up with you to make sure you have everything you need. Here's to your success and peace of mind! My staff and I will meet you at the back with the kits."

EXAMPLE #4

In a briefing-style meeting, design chief Jennie Berman speaks to her company's founders.

In her Great Closing Segment One, recall promises kept, she says:

"When we commenced today's briefing, I promised you would have a clear picture of our company's market position and have a reliable forecast of our position through the upcoming five years. Using the expert's analysis and the executive team's assessments, you saw for yourself how the technology roadmap and timeline play out. We pinpointed precisely where we are and examined the forecast that shows where we are headed."

In her Great Closing Segment Two, add unexpected value, she says:

"I'd like to offer a traditional route to pursuing more growth and revenue: discreetly looking at potential acquisition candidates. I have the profile on a very promising one here, with solid technology and owners who can invent but need our infrastructure and management. Would you like to see it?"

In her Great Closing Segment Three, give instructions, she says:

"Great. The next step is to pick up the phone and pay a visit to their offices. Let's do that while we're together now. Let's pick up the phone and arrange a visit with them."

EXAMPLE #5

Let's revisit the training and team meeting led by retail chain store owner Harry Harounian.

In his Great Closing Segment One, recall promises kept, he says:

"As I promised, you got the chance to compete for some great prizes. The first prize goes to the clerk who got all the clothes hung up in the fastest time: she wins an iPad. The second prize goes to the second-fastest clerk, who wins four tickets to an AMC theater with coupons for popcorn and sodas. The third prize goes to the clerk who had the third-fastest time. She wins a manicure and pedicure at our mall's beauty salon. Also, to emphasize that everyone can win by implementing this new system, there'll be pizza and sodas for everyone in the break room as soon as we finish today's training."

In his Great Closing Segment Two, add unexpected value, he says:

"I would like to offer you something more. Beginning tomorrow morning, you get the opportunity to win even better prizes. We're implementing a mystery shopper program for the next four weeks. On all shifts, evaluators who appear to be customers will visit the store, watching to see which clerks use the new system effectively. Plus, store management will be on the lookout as well. If a mystery shopper or store manager catches you 'doing it right,' meaning you are using the clean-up and re-rack system efficiently, you'll be awarded ten points on the spot. At the end of the month, we will award prizes to the top five individuals and top three teams with the most points. You can see on this board what team you're on, so you can coach each other and increase your chances of winning. Are you ready to win this contest?"

In his Great Closing Segment Three, give instructions, he says:

"Wonderful! Now we need your autograph. Here are the rules of the contest and the new policy for you to read and sign. Once again, sign the paper that has the contest rules and new policy."

EXAMPLE #6

In a persuasive-style meeting, software sales representative Tony Michaels speaks to decision-makers.

In his Great Closing Segment One, recall promises kept, he says:

"As I promised when we started this session, you are deciding if this software meets the most demanding aspects of your job. You gave valuable feedback on what the software must do, and you saw with your own eyes what it could do under your command. Of course, I'm delighted that your initial feedback is so positive."

In his Great Closing Segment Two, add unexpected value, he says:

"I want to offer you a challenge, a chance to see how you rank against all of our software users. Depending on your skill, you can win some great prizes. You'll find the rules and prizes on our company's website by logging on with the log-in codes you'll receive before you leave today. The challenge is this: It takes the average user 20 minutes to master the protocol in our package. If you can match that, you'll win a free subscription to one of many cool magazines listed on the prize page. Plus, if you can beat that, you can pick from a fantastic group of electronic gadgets. You'll see those on the prize page, too."

In his Great Closing Segment Three, give instructions, he says:

"You just need to log in. The software trial will start up onscreen with prompts that take you through it. Just remember, the clock starts as soon as you make your first keystroke. Would you like to compete with our other users because you can win prizes? You have the next three days to win, so log on before Thursday at 3 p.m. As you see me on the way out, I'm going to hand you your unique log-in code. The prizes will be available for the next three days, so put it on your calendar to log in and play before Thursday at 3 p.m. Remember, see me on your way out. I will hand you your unique log-in code for the website."

CLOSING IS EASY, NATURAL AND SUCCESSFUL

When you speak up and succeed, using the Speak Up System, you don't need any tricks, unfair tactics, bullying, pleading, or pestering to get what you want from every meeting, presentation, and conversation. You simply rely on the backbone of success, a reliable way to lead your audience to take action.

TAKE EVERY OPPORTUNITY TO BE A COMMUNICATION LEADER

You are always in collaboration with the people around you. The Speak Up System empowers you to engage and maximize these opportunities fully. You now have new insights, ideas, structure, examples, and a new sense of personal empowerment. It's time to use all that and enjoy the career and business success you deserve.

Speak up and succeed!

Appendix

Helpful Resources

Library of Success, Pg. 223

Four Dimensions of Decision-making Cheat Sheet, Pg. 229

More Assets, Pg. 235

Index, Pg. 237

Nance Speaks!

Library of Success

I N THIS SECTION, YOU SEE A CHART THAT OUTLINES A TYPICAL LIBRARY OF Success, which is the perfect way to organize all the content you need for presentations. Depending on how you need to access content, you might keep your content in computer files, in the cloud, on a spreadsheet, in a box on your floor, or even place it on a bookshelf. You might use an app like Evernote because it's easy to add and tag articles, visuals, reports, and even ideas there.

Be proactive. Read, write, create graphics, find multimedia, and collect material related to topics you expect to speak up about. The goal is to have useful, well-organized content ready before you need it, so you can quickly prepare for any meeting, presentation, or conversation.

On NanceSpeaks.com, there's a visual guide to the Library of Success, with definitions and examples. In this book's chapters on Act Two, Streamlined Content, you see which components work best for each segment. On the chart below, you can see which components are ideal for specific audiences and meeting styles. Most important for quick and easy preparation, you will find a two-digit code following each content component. When you brainstorm about a presentation, jot down the codes for the content you're considering. That speeds up your planning process! Preparation can take you ten minutes or less.

DUCK
Protector

HUMMINGBIRD
Delegator

OWL
Visionary

WOODPECKER
Analyst

PEACOCK
Trendsetter

Content Component	Bird	Persuasive	Training	Team	Briefing
		Interaction Styles			
ACCOUNTABILITY					
Budgets - BD	✳			•	•
Contracts - CN	✳				•
Forecasts - FO	✳	•		•	•
Letters of Agreement - LA	✳				•
Proposals - PA	✳	•			•
Roadmaps and Timelines - RT	✳	•	•	•	•
Specifications - SP	✳		•	•	•
Total Cost + Use Analysis - TC	✳	•			•
COMPARISONS					
Comparison of Alternative Courses of Action - CA	✳			•	•
Comparison of Competition - CC	✳	•			•
CREDIBILITY					
People Profiles - PF	✳			•	
References - RE	✳	•			
Testimonials + Endorsements - TE	✳	•			•
Third Party Standards + Evaluations - TH	✳	•	•	•	
DEMONSTRATIONS					
Features, Functions + Benefits - FB	✳	•	•		
Product Demonstrations - PR	✳	•	•		•
Proprietary Processes or Parts - PP	✳	•	•	•	•
Samples - SA	✳	•	•	•	•

Player Legend (Bird)

OWL ✳ **DUCK** ✳ **PEACOCK** ✳ **WOODPECKER** ✳ **HUMMINGBIRD** ✳

	Bird	Persuasive	Training	Team	Briefing
Interaction Styles					
DOWNSIDES					
Contrary Data or Conclusions - CD	✳				•
Plan Bs - PB	✳		•	•	•
Risk Analysis - RA	✳				•
INSIGHTS					
Analogies - AN	✳		•	•	
Examples - EX	✳	•	•	•	•
Graphics, Photos, Animation + Artwork - GA	✳	•	•	•	•
Props - PS	✳	•	•	•	
Recommendations - RC	✳	•			•
Resources - RS	✳		•	•	
Video + Audio - VA	✳	•	•	•	
INSPIRATION					
Invention + Discovery Stories - ID	✳	•	•		
Motivating Misery Trigger Stories - MM	✳	•	•	•	•
Rewards + Results Lists - RR	✳	•	•	•	•
Success Stories, Applications + Case Histories - SS	✳	•	•		

Player Legend (Bird)

OWL ✳ **DUCK** ✳ **PEACOCK** ✳ **WOODPECKER** ✳ **HUMMINGBIRD** ✳

	Bird	Interaction Styles			
		Persuasive	Training	Team	Briefing
INTERACTIVITY					
Assessments - AS	✳		•	•	
Audience Experiences - AE	✳	•	•	•	
Communication Facilitation - CF	✳	•	•	•	•
Hands-on Practice - HO	✳		•		
Premiums - PM	✳				
Questions + Answers: Question Guides - QA	✳	•	•	•	•
Questionnaires - QS	✳	•		•	
Role-Play - RP	✳		•	•	
LOGIC					
Blueprints or Technical Drawings - BT	✳		•	•	•
Data with Analysis - DD	✳	•	•	•	•
Facts + Figures, Charts - FF	✳			•	•
Technical Data - TD	✳		•	•	
TIPS					
Lists of Do's + Don'ts - LD	✳		•		
Step-By-Step Instructions - ST	✳		•		
Techniques, Advanced - TN	✳		•		
Tips, Secrets + Hints - TS	✳	•	•	•	•

Player Legend (Bird)

OWL ✳   DUCK ✳   PEACOCK ✳   WOODPECKER ✳   HUMMINGBIRD ✳

The Four Dimensions of Decision-Making

I N THIS SECTION VIEW YOUR "CHEAT SHEET" OF THE FOUR DIMENSIONS OF Decision-Making. This is another tool to help you quickly plan what you will say in a meeting, presentation, and conversation. Each dimension of decision-making enables you to choose the ideal content to use, and customize it based on your audience and the specific resistance you face. You also get rules for determining your ideal lead-off component and tips on vocal variety and using your time effectively.

These dimensions help you choose the ideal content components from your Library of Success and deliver them effectively.

DIMENSION 1: PLAYERS

In every audience, you have players. These are the very important people who play a significant role in your success or failure. After reviewing studies of 36,000 decision-makers, I've developed five "bird brain-styles" that accurately profile the players in your audiences. Once you recognize them, it's easy to choose content that aligns with each player's personality, priorities, and preferences.

I've named these player profiles after five types of birds, to make them easy for you to remember. They are Owls, Ducks, Peacocks, Hummingbirds, and Woodpeckers. I bet just from hearing these names; you can guess their characteristics and content preferences. Let's see if you are correct.

OWLS ARE WISE AND VISIONARY

They ask questions like, "How does your proposal reflect our mission and values?"

They want to see strategic, long-term plans and forecasts of future performance.

DUCKS ARE FOLLOWERS

They ask questions like, "What is the most orderly way to implement your proposal?"

They respond positively when your recommendations are based on conventional rules and success stories.

PEACOCKS ARE SHOWY, BIG IDEA PEOPLE

They ask questions like, "How will your proposal set us apart and get us visibility?"

They respond to invention and discovery stories, supported by highly visual content.

HUMMINGBIRDS ARE IMPATIENT

They ask questions like, "How quickly can you tell me the benefits of your proposal?"

They like tips and examples to get up-to-speed quickly.

WOODPECKERS LIKE TO DRILL DOWN ON DETAILS

They ask questions like, "Where is the source material so I can verify the conclusions in your proposal?"

They like data with analysis and technical drawings.

DIMENSION 2: INTERACTION STYLES

In the Speak Up System, you use four meeting styles to create specific transformations in your players' mindsets. The styles are persuasive, training, team-building, and briefing. How do you choose? Identify the emotional basis of your players' resistance to taking action. Think about why a player might have objections to your solution. Strategically use content to overcome each type of resistance.

Persuasive-style Interactions

Perhaps players had a bad experience or previous failure that haunts them. Transform players who are negative or indifferent to feeling positive and enthusiastic. You'll succeed with content from your credibility and insights sections.

Training-style Interactions

Players may lack confidence in their ability to understand or use what you recommend. Transform players from feeling incompetent or uncertain to proficient and confident. Training should include components from your interactivity and tips sections.

Team-style Interactions

Players might be self-centered and not connected to the group goal. Transform players who feel disconnected or self-centered to being unified and group goal-oriented. Build team spirit with components from your inspiration and comparisons sections.

Briefing-style Interactions

Players might be missing an essential piece of information that would help them understand and then feel eager to take action as you desire. Transform players who feel stuck or partially informed to being updated and proactive. When you haven't been able to get approval or the go-ahead: provide content from your accountability and logic sections.

DIMENSION 3: YOUR IDEAL LEAD-OFF COMPONENT

The essential component should start each segment of Act Two. How do you determine which component is ideal? Here are the criteria.

1. **Fresh:** deliver new or surprising information.
2. **Significant:** provide relevant, applicable, or important content.
3. **Sensitive:** present content that communicates your compassion and respect.

DIMENSION 4: ORCHESTRATION

Vary your pitch, pace, and volume to increase the emotional response to each content component. The sound of your words acts like a movie's musical score. Here are some examples.

1. When you deliver step-by-step instructions, slow your pace so players can easily follow you.
2. When you introduce your ideal lead-off component, be lively and uplifting.
3. When you tell a success story, raise your volume and pitch to express excitement.

How should you allocate time for each act of the SPEAK UP SYSTEM? While your needs might vary for a particular topic or audience, a good general formula for using time is:

Act One, Your Great Opening = 15%
Act Two, Your Streamlined Content = 70%
Act Three, Your Great Closing = 15%

Remember, you'll find more guidance and information at NanceSpeaks.com.

More Assets

CONGRATULATIONS!

You are ready to become a communication leader! You have the key concepts and backbone of success, which is the SPEAK UP SYSTEM. You have a way to develop your own Library of Success so you have the right content ready to plan your next presentation. Plus, you have the Four Dimensions of Decision-making to help you select and deliver that content powerfully.

You are ready to get what you want in any meeting, presentation, or conversation. It's time to speak up and succeed!

If you want more guidance, resources, inspiration, and a community of like-minded individuals and organizations, please join me at NanceSpeaks.com.

APPENDIX

Index

A

Accountability 49, 50, 51, 53, 55, 99,
    130, 131, 137, 185, 188, 233
Act One
  Segment One 49, 50, 51, 53, 55, 99,
    130, 131, 137, 185, 188, 233
  Segment Three 49, 50, 51, 53, 55, 99,
    130, 131, 137, 185, 188, 233
  Segment Two 49, 50, 51, 53, 55, 99,
    130, 131, 137, 185, 188, 233
Act Three
  Segment One 49, 50, 51, 53, 55, 99,
    130, 131, 137, 185, 188, 233
  Segment Three 49, 50, 51, 53, 55, 99,
    130, 131, 137, 185, 188, 233
  Segment Two 49, 50, 51, 53, 55, 99,
    130, 131, 137, 185, 188, 233
Act Two
  Segment One 49, 50, 51, 53, 55, 99,
    130, 131, 137, 185, 188, 233
  Segment Three 49, 50, 51, 53, 55, 99,
    130, 131, 137, 185, 188, 233
  Segment Two 49, 50, 51, 53, 55, 99,
    130, 131, 137, 185, 188, 233
Ambition 98
Anthony, Susan B. 68
As I promised 187, 216, 218

B

Bazin, Serena 205
Briefing iii, 20, 58, 61, 63, 101, 105, 139,
    140, 188, 231

C

Career Transition 13
Carnegie, Andrew 66
CASA 66, 68
Cheng, Maya 71
Coca-Cola Company 1, 197, 241
Communicate Your Philosophy 103
Communication Leadership iii, 3, 8,
    12, 23, 26
Comparisons 49, 50, 51, 53, 55, 99, 130,
    131, 137, 185, 188, 233
Compassionate mindset 24
Craving 30, 31, 32
Create Belief 46, 50, 53, 64, 72, 78, 84
Creativity 98
Credibility 49, 50, 51, 53, 55, 99, 130,
    131, 137, 185, 188, 233
Crime Story 49, 50, 51, 53, 55, 99, 130,
    131, 137, 185, 188, 233

D

Demonstrations 49, 50, 51, 53, 55, 99,
    130, 131, 137, 185, 188, 233
Depth Deficit 29
Dissatisfaction Gap 29
Downsides 49, 50, 51, 53, 55, 99, 130,
    131, 137, 185, 188, 233
Dramatic Quotation 49, 50, 51, 53, 55,
    99, 130, 131, 137, 185, 188, 233
Ducks 224, 230

E

Epidemic Statistic 49, 50, 51, 53, 55, 99, 130, 131, 137, 185, 188, 233
Ewig, Sam 77

F

Fear 30, 31, 32
Foster Understanding 46, 50, 53, 64, 72, 78, 84
Four Dimensions of Decision-making 221, 235

G

Ghost Conversation 37
Goldilocks 34, 163, 198
Great Closing 47, 49, 50, 51, 53, 54, 55, 67, 68, 74, 79, 85, 86, 99, 130, 131, 135, 137, 140, 141, 142, 143, 144, 146, 175, 181, 185, 187, 188, 189, 190, 193, 195, 196, 197, 198, 201, 202, 203, 204, 205, 211, 212, 213, 214, 216, 217, 218, 219, 233, 238
Great Opening 49, 50, 51, 53, 55, 99, 130, 131, 137, 185, 188, 233

H

Heroic Achievement 49, 50, 51, 53, 55, 99, 130, 131, 137, 185, 188, 233
Hummingbirds 224, 230

I

Ignite Urgency 46, 50, 53, 64, 72, 78, 84
Individuality 98
Insights 49, 50, 51, 53, 55, 99, 130, 131, 137, 185, 188, 233
Inspiration 49, 50, 51, 53, 55, 99, 130, 131, 137, 185, 188, 233

Intangible Gifts 49, 50, 51, 53, 55, 99, 130, 131, 137, 185, 188, 233
Interaction Styles 231
Interactivity 49, 50, 51, 53, 55, 99, 130, 131, 137, 185, 188, 233
I started off with the guarantee 187

L

Lead-off Component 232
Let's see if you got 187
Library of Success v, 36, 53, 54, 59, 139, 140, 151, 153, 156, 161, 163, 164, 166, 167, 173, 175, 177, 178, 221, 223, 229, 235
Lipton, Jennifer 204
Logic 49, 50, 51, 53, 55, 99, 130, 131, 137, 185, 188, 233

M

Misery iii, 8, 29, 30, 31, 33, 167, 168
Misery Triggers iii, 8, 29
My commitment to you 135, 187

N

Nugget 49, 50, 51, 53, 55, 99, 130, 131, 137, 185, 188, 233

O

Orchestration 233
Outcome Mind 17, 18
Owls 224, 230

P

Pain 30, 31
Parinello, Anthony ix
PAW 38, 39, 212, 215
Peacocks 224, 230
Personal Brand Triad 19, 36

Persuasive iii, 20, 58, 61, 63, 101, 105, 139, 140, 188, 231

Players 59, 61, 75, 84, 85, 103, 139, 144, 188, 197, 198, 202, 205, 211, 212, 213, 230, 231, 233

Progressive Outcomes 21

Promises 49, 50, 51, 53, 55, 99, 130, 131, 137, 185, 188, 233

R

Reciprocity 25, 47, 55

Reiko 196

Relationship Map 21

Ride 196

S

Sagan, Carl 67

Security 98

Shankman, Peter i

Showcase Your Values 104

Speak Up System iii, iv, 1, 4, 5, 7, 9, 12, 13, 14, 15, 21, 22, 25, 26, 28, 33, 36, 41, 42, 43, 45, 49, 50, 56, 57, 59, 62, 70, 76, 82, 87, 91, 99, 148, 151, 180, 181, 190, 219, 231, 233, 235

Startling Statistic 49, 50, 51, 53, 55, 99, 130, 131, 137, 185, 188, 233

Streamlined Content 49, 50, 51, 53, 55, 99, 130, 131, 137, 185, 188, 233

Success vii, xi, 1, 2, 3, 4, 5, 9, 11, 12, 13, 15, 18, 19, 21, 32, 33, 37, 49, 51, 55, 59, 74, 85, 86, 99, 100, 117, 118, 125, 127, 128, 129, 130, 164, 168, 188, 198, 205, 215, 217, 219, 230, 233, 235, 241

Success Story 49, 50, 51, 53, 55, 99, 130, 131, 137, 185, 188, 233

Surprising Analogy 124

Surprising Example 124

T

Tangible Gifts 49, 50, 51, 53, 55, 99, 130, 131, 137, 185, 188, 233

Team iii, 20, 58, 61, 63, 101, 105, 139, 140, 188, 231

Testimonials 166, 187

Tips 49, 50, 51, 53, 55, 99, 130, 131, 137, 185, 188, 233

Training iii, 20, 58, 61, 63, 101, 105, 139, 140, 188, 231

Transformation Channel 50, 151, 161, 175, 181, 185, 209

Trigger Talk 35, 36

V

Vitality 98

W

Woodpeckers 224, 230

About Nance Rosen

CNBC named Nance Rosen, the "Top Job Coach." She is a member of the elite Forbes Coaches Council. Investor's Business Daily featured her in its Managing for Success column. Over 420 media outlets feature Nance on business communication, careers, personal branding, and business success.

She's a former marketing executive with The Coca-Cola Company, the number one most recognized brand in the world.

She hosted International Business on Public Radio and NightCap on television, where she spoke to the world's most important people in business, politics, labor, and government. The first woman director of marketing in the Global 2000 technology sector, past president of the Medical Marketing Association, Nance is now a successful serial entrepreneur, educator, and coach.

Nance is CEO of Nance Speaks! and New Career Planning. She produced a Wall Street Journal bestseller, BusinessWeek bestseller and the number one sales book on Amazon. Nance is the author of *Speak Up & Succeed: How to get everything you want in meetings, presentations and conversations.* Her upcoming book is *Billion Dollar Personal Branding: How to Avoid 10 Killer Mistakes and Live the Life of Your Dreams.*

Nance is a world-class speaker and educator at UCLAx and universities around the world. Her corporate clients include Disney, Red Bull, Ingram Micro, Entrepreneur's Organization, and other prestige firms. She is a business and career coach for success-minded clients at ATT, Boingo, Sony, Microsoft and other employers, and those seeking career transitions. She consults on business development with entrepreneurs and communication with non-profit organizations.

Nance has created the personal branding for some of the world's most famous celebrities, high profile business people, and well-known coaches and speakers.

For additional examples and info,
or to contact Nance, visit

NanceSpeaks.com